D1200359

IMMIGRANTS IN AMERICA

Chinese Americans

German Americans

Irish Americans

Italian Americans

Japanese Americans

Swedish Americans

Swedish
AMERICANS

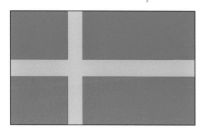

Cory Gideon Gunderson

CHELSEA HOUSE
PUBLISHERS
A Haights Cross Communications Company

Philadelphia

Frontispiece: Map of Sweden with world map inset. Swedish immigrants braved a long and harsh journey across the Altantic Ocean for a new and better life in America.

Dedication: With thanks to Judith Gustafson, a Swedish American who served as an invaluable resource in my research of this book.

CHELSEA HOUSE PUBLISHERS

VP, New Product Development Sally Cheney
Director of Production Kim Shinners
Creative Manager Takeshi Takahashi
Manufacturing Manager Diann Grasse

Staff for SWEDISH AMERICANS

Assistant Editor Kate Sullivan
Production Editor Jaimie Winkler
Picture Researcher Pat Holl
Series Designer Takeshi Takahashi
Cover Designer Takeshi Takahashi
Layout 21st Century Publishing and Communications, Inc.

A Haights Cross Communications ◄─ Company

http://www.chelseahouse.com

First Printing

1 3 5 7 9 8 6 4 2

Library of Congress Cataloging-in-Publication Data

Gunderson, Cory Gideon.
   Swedish Americans / Cory Gideon Gunderson.
      p. cm.—(Immigrants in America)
Includes bibliographical references (p.) and index.
   ISBN 0-7910-7131-6HC   0-7910-7514-1PB
   1. Swedish Americans—History—Juvenile literature. 2. Immigrants—United States—History—Juvenile literature. 3. Sweden—Emigration and immigration—History—Juvenile literature. 4. United States—Emigration and immigration—History—Juvenile literature. [1. Swedish Americans. 2. Immigrants.] I. Title. II. Series: Immigrants in America (Chelsea House Publishers)
E184.S23 G86 2003
973'.04397—dc21

                                                    2002151609

CONTENTS

Introduction
Daniel Patrick Moynihan   6

1 The Swedes in America   12

2 The Old Country   20

3 America Fever   30

4 Tamers of the Frontier   44

5 Social Issues in
   Industrial America   56

6 Swedish Identity
   Across the Atlantic   68

7 Into the Melting Pot:
   The Swedish–American Influence   84

Chronology   94
Bibliography   96
Further Reading   97
Websites   98
Organizations   99
Index   100

A NATION OF NATIONS

Daniel Patrick Moynihan

The Constitution of the United States begins: "We the People of the United States . . ." Yet, as we know, the United States was not then and is not now made up of a single group. It is made up of many peoples. Immigrants and bondsmen from Europe, Asia, the Pacific Islands, Africa, and Central and South America came here or were brought here, and still they come. They forged one nation and made it their own. More than 100 years ago, Walt Whitman expressed this great central fact of America: "Here is not merely a nation, but a teeming Nation of nations."

Although the ingenuity and acts of courage of these immigrants, our ancestors, shaped the North American way of life, we sometimes take their contributions for granted. This fine series, IMMIGRANTS IN AMERICA, examines the experiences and contributions of different immigrant groups and how these contributions determined the future of the United States and Canada.

Immigrants did not abandon their ethnic traditions when they reached the shores of North America. Each ethnic group had its own customs and traditions, and each brought different experiences, accomplishments, skills, values, styles of dress, and tastes in food that lingered long after its arrival. Yet this profusion of differences created a bond among immigrants. Ethnic foods, for example, sometimes became "typically" American, such as frankfurters, pizzas, and tacos.

The United States and Canada are unusual in this respect. Whereas religious and ethnic differences have sparked intolerance throughout the rest of the world, North Americans have struggled to learn how to respect each other's differences and live in harmony.

Our two countries are hardly the only two in which different groups must learn to live together. There is no nation of significant size anywhere in the world that would not be classified as multiethnic. But only in North America are there so *many* different groups, most of them living cheek by jowl with one another.

This is not easy. Look around the world. And it has not always been easy for us. Witness the exclusion of Chinese immigrants, and for practical purposes the Japanese also, in the late nineteenth century. But by the late twentieth century, Chinese and Japanese Americans were the most successful of all the groups recorded by the census. We have had prejudice aplenty, but it has been resisted and recurrently overcome.

The remarkable ability of Americans to live together as one people was seriously threatened by the issue of slavery. Thousands of settlers from the British Isles had arrived in the colonies as indentured servants, agreeing to work for a specified number of years on farms or as apprentices in return for passage to America and room and board. When the first Africans arrived in the then-British colonies during the seventeenth century, some colonists thought that they, too, should be treated as indentured servants. Eventually, the question of whether the Africans should be treated as indentured, like the English, or as slaves who could be owned for life, was considered in a Maryland court. The court's calamitous decree held that blacks were slaves bound to a lifelong servitude, and so also were their children. America went through a time of moral examination and civil war before African slaves and their descendants were finally freed. The principle that all people are created equal had faced its greatest challenge and it survived.

Yet the court ruling that set blacks apart from other races fanned flames of discrimination that burned long after slavery was abolished—and that still flicker today. Indeed, it was about the time of the American Civil War that European theories of evolution were turned to the service of ranking different peoples by their presumed distance from our apelike ancestors!

When the Irish flooded American cities to escape the famine in Ireland, the cartoonists caricatured the typical "Paddy" (a common term for Irish immigrants) as an apelike creature with jutting jaw and sloping forehead.

By the twentieth century, racism and ethnic prejudice had given rise to virulent theories of a Northern European master race. When Adolf Hitler came to power in Germany in 1933, he popularized the notion of an Aryan race. Only a man of the deepest ignorance and evil could have done this. *Aryan* is a Sanskrit word taken from the ancient language of the civilizations that inhabited the Indus Valley, which now includes Pakistan and much of Northern India. The term "Aryan," which means "noble," was first used by the eminent German linguist Max Müller to denote the Indo-European family of languages. Müller was horrified that anyone could think of it in terms of a race of blond-haired, blue-eyed Teutons. But the Nazis embraced the notion of a master race. Anyone with darker and heavier features was considered inferior. Buttressed by these theories, the German Nazi state from 1933 to 1945 set out to destroy European Jews, along with Poles, Gypsies, Russians, and other groups considered inferior. They nearly succeeded. Millions of these people were murdered.

The tragedies brought on by ethnic and racial intolerance throughout the world demonstrate the importance of North America's efforts to create a society free of prejudice and inequality.

A relatively recent example of the New World's desire to resolve ethnic friction nonviolently is the solution that the Canadians found to a conflict between two ethnic groups. A long-standing dispute as to whether Canadian culture was properly English or properly French resurfaced in the mid-1960s, dividing the peoples of the French-speaking Province of Quebec from those of the English-speaking provinces. Relations grew tense, then bitter, then violent. The Royal Commission on Bilingualism and Biculturalism was established to study the growing crisis and to propose measures to ease the tensions. As a result of the commission's recommendations, all official documents and statements from the national government's capital at Ottawa are now issued in both French and English, and bilingual education is encouraged. But the commissioners recorded that there were many other groups as well.

Toward the end of the nineteenth century in the United States, public figures such as Theodore Roosevelt began speaking about "Americanism," deploring "hyphenated Americans" as persons only partly assimilated—later it would be said insufficiently loyal—to their adopted country. Ethnicity was seen by many as a threat to national cohesion, and even to national security. During World War I, referring to German Americans, Roosevelt would speak of "the Hun within." During World War II, immigrant Germans and Italians were classified as "enemy aliens," and Japanese Americans were settled in detention camps. With time, however, we became more accepting as ethnicity emerged as a *form* of Americanism, celebrated in the annual Columbus Day and Steuben Day parades, the West Indian parade, the Pakistani parade, and in New York City the venerable St. Patrick's Day parade, which dates back before the American Revolution.

In time, the Bureau of the Census took note. In 1980, for the first time, the census questionnaire asked, "What is this person's ancestry?" In parentheses, it stated: "For example: Afro-American, English, French, German" and so on through a list of 16 possibilities, followed by "etc." The results were a bit misleading. Remember, it was a new question. Census officials now speculate that because the first European group listed was English, many respondents simply stopped there. The result was an "overcount." By 2000, however, the bureau was getting better.

The 2000 Census also asked people to identify their ancestry. More than 80 percent chose one or more groups from a list of 89 different groups. Most people "specified," as the Census states, a "single ancestry," but almost a quarter cited "multiple ancestry." So which is it: are we a melting pot or a "Nation of nations"? The answer is both. Americans share a common citizenship, which is the most important fact of our civic life. But most also feel part of one group or another, especially recent arrivals.

Of which there are many indeed! Since 1970 more than 26 million immigrants have entered the United States; most immigrants have entered legally, but of late not all. For the longest time, anyone could enter. Under the Constitution, drawn up in 1797, even the trade in African slaves was protected for 20 years—a hideous practice, but well established in Southern states. In time, however, hostility toward newcomers appeared, notably tinged with racial fears. In 1882 an act of U.S. Congress excluded further Chinese immigration, responding to pressure from Californians anxious about "cheap labor." Next there was agitation to exclude Japanese, which only ended when the Japanese government, in what was termed a "Gentleman's Agreement," consented to withhold passports from Japanese emigrants. Restrictions on Asians continued until 1965.

Indeed, at the end of the nineteenth century there was much talk about the "Anglo-Saxon race" and its many virtues. The United States had reached an informal alliance with Great Britain, and we were setting up an empire of our own that included the Philippines, Cuba, Puerto Rico, and Hawaii. Weren't we different from those "others"? Not exactly. Migration has been going on across the world from the beginning of time and there is no such thing as a pure race. The humorist Finley Peter Dunne wrote: "An Anglo-Saxon…is a German that's forgot who was his parents." Indeed, following the departure of the Romans from Britain in the year A.D. 410, Germanic tribes, including Saxons from northern Germany and Anglos from southern Denmark, migrated into the British Isles. In time they defined what we now call Britain, driving the Celts to Wales and Ireland, with an essentially Celtic Scotland to the north.

Thus immigrants from the British Isles, approximately a third of the present day population of the United States, were already a heterogeneous group. Perhaps even more importantly, they belonged to many different religious denominations including the Puritan, Congregational, Episcopalian, Quaker, and Catholic churches, and even a small community of Sephardic Jews from Brazil! No group made up a majority; religious toleration came about largely because there seemed to be no alternative.

American immigration policy developed in much this way. Though completely open at the beginning, over time, efforts were made to limit the influx of certain immigrant groups, in the manner of the exclusion of Asians in the late nineteenth century and the Southern Europeans by the early twentieth century. By the 1960s, however, America was already too diverse to pretend otherwise, and immigration was opened to all nations.

The people of North America are the descendants of one of the greatest migrations in history. And that migration is not over. Koreans, Vietnamese, Mexicans, Nicaraguans, Pakistanis, Indians, Arabs, and many others are heading for the shores of North America in large numbers. This mix of cultures shapes every aspect of our lives. To understand ourselves, we must know something about our diverse ethnic ancestry. Nothing so defines the North American nations as the motto on the Great Seal of the United States: *E Pluribus Unum*—Out of Many, One. ■

1 THE SWEDES IN AMERICA

To us America was a land of milk and honey, so spurred on by the illusions of fairy tales, we left the meager board Venjan had afforded us for the faraway promised land. We were facing starvation as there had been several consecutive years of crop failure, due mostly to poor soil and early frosts, and there was not enough food in Venjan to feed its inhabitants.

Olof Olson, Swedish emigrant, in 1938;
recounting life in his village, Venjan, in 1869

Sweden's grain crop rotted in 1867 under heavy rainfall that growing season. The next year's crops burned because of too little rain. Starvation weakened many Swedes who had gone hungry too long, and the third consecutive year of crop failure in 1869 created unbearable conditions. Disease claimed the lives

The history of Swedish immigration to America dates as far back as 1638, when a small group established "New Sweden" in what is now the state of Delaware. This depiction shows Native Americans greeting these early Swedish settlers as they came ashore.

of thousands of Swedes too vulnerable to resist it. In those three years, known as the "starvation years," close to 60,000 fled this devastation in search of a better life in America.

These Swedes were not the first to leave their homeland in search of a better life across the Atlantic. In 1638, about

18 years after the Mayflower landed in America, the first Swedish immigrants established a colony in what is now known as the state of Delaware. New Sweden was settled in 1638 under the direction and control of the government in Stockholm. But from the 1700s until the early 1800s, the Swedish government restricted its citizens from leaving their country.

Between 1750 and 1850, Sweden's population doubled and then continued to increase. This phenomenon was attributed to "peace, vaccination, and potatoes," according to Esaias Tegne'r, a Swedish bishop and poet. Sweden had not been at war since 1814. The infant mortality rate had dropped from 21 percent in 1750 to 15 percent in 1850, and potatoes had been introduced to the country as a nutritious supplement to feed the hungry. This population trend created much pressure on the land. With only one-tenth of Sweden's land being well suited for farming, the country increasingly had difficulty supporting its inhabitants. By the mid 1800s, the Swedish government saw the emigration of its citizens as a benefit to its country, that is, as a way to lessen Sweden's obligations. New laws were created that freed the Swedish people to leave for America

Between 1850 and 1921, well over one million Swedes left their homeland to begin a new life in America. All of the emigrants had hopes for a better life, but their reasons for leaving and their final destinations varied.

THE PHASES OF SWEDISH IMMIGRATION

The early phase of Swedish immigrants (1840–1864) were neither wealthy nor poor. They chose to flee from the land that could no longer sustain the growing masses. Some sought religious freedom from the state-run Lutheran Church. Others turned their backs on a government that ruled their lives and categorized them by class. Still others were motivated by dreams of striking it rich in a gold rush. Many sought to own land in their new home, something they were unable to do in Sweden. President Lincoln's Homestead Act of 1862 opened up opportunities for newly arrived immigrants to American to obtain

Swedish Immigration in Numbers

Swedish Immigration to the United States, 1821–2000. Courtesy of the United States Immigration and Naturalization Service.

Note that the data for Norway and Sweden was not counted separately until 1871. The figures until 1871 include both countries' immigration statistics.

Decade	Number of Immigrants
1821–1830	91
1831–1840	1,201
1841–1850	13,903
1851–1860	20,931
1861–1870	109,298
1871–1880	95,323
1881–1890	176,586
1891–1900	226,266
1901–1910	249,534
1911–1920	95,074
1921–1930	97,249
1931–1940	3,960
1941–1950	10,665
1951–1960	21,697
1961–1970	17,116
1971–1980	6,531
1981–1990	11,018
1991–2000	12,715
TOTAL	1,404,947

160 acres of free land. Immigrants in this time frame typically traveled in large groups and tamed the frontier, developing the first Swedish settlements across Iowa, Minnesota, and Illinois. They paved the way for future immigrants.

Many immigrants in the next phase of immigration (1865–1889) fled from the hunger they endured in Sweden. Beyond the crop failures of the late 1860s, the late 1870s saw a new crisis. Wheat imported from other countries drove down the price of cereal grown in Sweden. With transportation to the United States now faster and more affordable and Swedish farmers unable to compete with the imported wheat, Swedish emigration soared. Swedish farmers typically settled in the Midwest so they could continue farming. Laborers moved to large cities in Illinois, Minnesota, and Michigan, where they could get jobs working in iron mines or in the building industry, or where they'd follow the westward expansion to get jobs with the railroad or with lumber companies. Many farmers needed these same jobs to supplement their income in the off-season. Single Swedish girls moved to cities where middle-class American families hired them as maids. Group emigration became less necessary, since immigrants could frequently meet up with Swedish-American friends or relatives who had emigrated before them.

The third wave of immigrants (1890–1914) included more young, single adults than in the decades before. Young men chose to leave their Swedish homeland before they were forced into military service. Many of these immigrants were urban, industrial workers who came because the United States economy afforded them higher wages than they could earn in their native land.

From the 1870s, Chicago and the state of Minnesota became cradles of Swedish-American culture. The Swedes had their own newspapers, clubs, schools, and churches. The immigrants in these tightly knit communities could live their entire lives without speaking anything but their own Swedish language.

How Others Saw Them

An article in the December 1887 *Chautauquan*, a magazine covering contemporary issues, praised the Scandinavians as "Aryans, Protestants, and almost ideal pioneer farmers. They come from the early home of the English-speaking races, to freshen and re-inforce the American stock. They are a wholesome, virile race."

An American magazine article in the early 1900s stated, " 'Tis a simple fact, not flattery, that prosperity follows the Swedes. They are never lazy and very seldom unskilled. They mix brains with muscle. No people produces a smaller proportion of drudgers or kickers. They go about their work with a vim and cheerfulness whether the pay envelope is thick or thin—they have won the highest respect of all other Americans by deserving it. They are honest, industrious, wholesome people. There is not a Swedish slum in any American city. In morality and intelligence they rank with the best of us. . . . "

From a letter written by the governor of Illinois regarding the Swedish-American volunteers from the 55th Illinois: "the most efficient and most soldierly in the army."

The president of the Lake Superior and Mississippi Railroad reported to the stockholders, "These people [73 newly immigrated Swedes] are now comfortably fixed in the new homes, and, with restored health, are writing very encouraging letters to their friends and relatives in Sweden of the climate of Minnesota, the generosity of our company, etc. which will alone no doubt repay all the labor and money expended."

During a debate on immigration in the Senate in 1929, U.S. Senator Wheeler of Montana said, "I have listened with surprise to some of the statements made during this debate. One of the senators said, if I am not mistaken, that we have acquired the habit of allowing alien slackers to come into our country. I would like to know who these persons so referred to really are. Is it possibly the Swedes, the Norwegians, the Danes, or the Irish that are meant? Is it these people the speaker refers to? If my memory does not entirely fail me—and I served as U.S. district attorney in my state during the war—there was no more patriotic class of citizens than that composed of Swedes, Norwegians, and Danes."

Professor Babcock of the University of Minnesota wrote in *The Forum* in September 1892: "Certainly no class makes greater effort than the Scandinavians to become naturalized; none enters upon the rights and duties of American citizenship with more enthusiasm or honest, intelligent appreciation of its high privileges."

During the late 1800s, Minnesota and the Chicago area became well-established centers of Swedish-American culture. In these close-knit communities, Swedes established their own newspapers, churches, schools, and clubs. Here, Swedish-American children wear traditional clothing at a small-town dance in Minnesota in 1942.

For decades, Swedish Americans were able to keep their language and culture alive in the United States.

The Swedish exodus (mass departure) hit its peak around 1910, when 1.4 million Swedish immigrants were counted as United States citizens. With Sweden's population at 5.5 million at the time, this meant that about one-fifth of the world's Swedes claimed America as home. By 1930, Swedish Americans had settled in the western, middle-western, northeastern, and southern regions of the United States, though very few settled in the Deep South.

World War I created an aversion in America to everything considered foreign. Unfortunately, this led to the gradual loss of a cultural Swedish America. Today more than 4.5 million Americans claim Swedish ancestry. Some have observed that the newer generations of Swedish Americans are showing a renewed interest in learning more about their ancestors who journeyed across the Atlantic to clear forests, lay miles of railroad track, and build log homes or sod houses on the frontier. They want to know more about their ancestors, who were credited with having built entire cities in America, the land of milk and honey.

2

THE OLD COUNTRY

I had to go out and earn my bread already at the age of eight. Most of what I did was to look after children. Had to get up at four o'clock in the morning with the others. . . . I did not have time to go to school very much. I had to learn catechism, naturally, and that I had to do during the time I was watching the cows or some child. But I was not allowed to neglect Sunday school, for they wanted to drill into us poor people certain Biblical passages such as "Be godly and let us be contented," and so forth. . . . So passed the days of my childhood. . . . But whichever way I turned things, the future looked just as dark. Still I had to struggle along five more years before I could be considered a proper hired girl and get any wage.

M. M., North Dakota, from Värmlands, Sweden

Sweden is Europe's fourth-largest nation, and is dotted with spectacular lakes, mountains, and pine forests. The midsection of the country is rich in iron ore, and its southern regions provide fertile farmland. With only one-tenth of Sweden's overall land suitable for farming, and a dramatic population increase during the 1800s, however, many Swedes found it necessary to set their sights on a new and better life—in America.

PHYSICAL FEATURES AND LANGUAGE

Sweden is situated in the far northwestern part of Europe. Along with Norway to Sweden's north and west, it forms the Scandinavian Peninsula. To the northeast of Sweden is Finland, and Denmark is located off Sweden's southern-most border. The Gulf of Bothnia and the Baltic Sea meet Sweden's eastern coastline. The islands of Oland and Gotland in the Baltic Sea also belong to Sweden.

As Europe's fourth-largest country, Sweden's area is 173,732 square miles (449,964 square kilometers). Stockholm, the country's capital, is also its largest city. The northernmost part of Sweden is covered with lakes and mountains. The source of many rivers, falls, and rapids that flow to the Gulf of Bothnia can be traced to these mountains. Forests of Norway spruces and Scotch pines blanket the middle and southern parts of Sweden. Many rivers and the largest lakes in the country are located on this fairly level land. Rich deposits of iron ore are found in Sweden's midsection, whereas its most fertile, agricultural area is located to the south.

The Swedish language has its roots in the Germanic languages. Danish tongue, a development of a Germanic language, was spoken in Sweden and all the Scandinavian countries before the early Middle Ages. The Swedish branch of this language developed into its own unique language around 900–1500. It was called Old Swedish. Latin and Greek words found their way into the Swedish language when Christianity came to the country. French and German words are also part of modern Swedish.

EARLY SWEDISH HISTORY

Details of Sweden's history before the tenth century are unclear. Sweden and other northern European countries have battled against each other and against continental European powers for hundreds of years. Large pieces of Sweden's land have been lost to other countries and some regained.

Sweden's pagan Nordic religion lasted into the 1100s, and the missionary Saint Ansgar brought Catholicism, the first Christian religion in Sweden, in 829. The Frankish missionaries who spread Christian teachings eventually established this religion in the eleventh century.

From the 800s until the 1000s, Swedish Vikings established colonies and trade routes in Russia and in eastern European countries. Sweden's power as a nation was strengthened under the reign of Eric IX from 1150 to 1160. Eric was killed by an enemy while attending Mass and later became Sweden's patron saint.

During the late 1200s, the crown first became firmly established as the ultimate authority over its citizens. This central government imposed laws and ordinances that governed the entire kingdom. King Magnus Ladulas organized Sweden's society in 1280 based on the feudal system. In this system, the king would give land to the noblemen who followed him and supplied him with soldiers in war times. These nobles then would give pieces of their land to the lower-class knights and lords who supported the nobles. The peasants had very little land and almost no rights. They were merely toilers of the land owned by the upper class.

Beginning in the mid 1300s, Sweden had a strong agriculturally based economy. However, when the Black Death, a form of bubonic plague, reached Sweden in 1350, the population decreased and abandoned farms were commonplace. The increase in iron production in the late 1400s enabled the country to rebuild its economy.

In 1389, Sweden came under the rule of Margaret I, who was queen of Norway and Denmark. Margaret's son, Erik of Pomerania, eventually became king and formed the Kalmar Union in 1397, which united the three kingdoms under his rule. This union lasted for over 100 years. Denmark's governing council stripped Erik of his power in 1438. The next year Sweden followed suit. To ward off future attempts by absolute rulers to gain control over them, the Swedish council formed a legislative body called the Riksdag. This move spread governing power over four houses: nobles, clergy, townspeople or burghers, and yeoman.

EARLY CONFLICTS AND BATTLES

Despite these government reforms, the Swedish people remained dissatisfied. When a rebellion seemed imminent, King Christian of Denmark (Kristian) II invaded Sweden in an effort to maintain his power over all three Scandinavian countries. He ordered the killing of many of his enemies; these murders became known as the Bloodbath of Stockholm.

The slaughter triggered a rebellion led by Gustav Vasa in 1521. With the rebellion's success, Gustav became administrator and then, in 1523, king of an independent Sweden. Gustav agreed with Martin Luther, a Catholic monk, that the Roman Catholic Church had too much centralized power. As king, he took the Catholic Church's property and diverted its money into his country's treasury. He appointed himself head of the Church of Sweden and ruled that the clergy must report to the king. Lutheranism was established as the state religion in 1527. No other religious beliefs were allowed for hundreds of years. Sweden prospered under Gustav's reign. The crown's power became even stronger in 1544, when Sweden introduced a hereditary monarchy.

In 1632, Gustav's grandson, King Gustav II Adolph, was killed in battle. Gustav II Adolph's daughter, six-year-old Christina, was the only remaining heir to the crown. Count Axel Oxenstierna, who had served as chancellor, led the Swedish government. In 1638, the Swedish government sent the first emigrants to America. These emigrants were to establish an international trade route and colony. New Sweden, the trading outpost on the Delaware Bay, was unprofitable. Though many of these immigrants stayed in America, further colonization there would not be pursued until almost 200 years later, when conditions in Sweden made it necessary.

In 1521, Gustav I became the first leader of an independent Sweden. Aligning his thoughts about the Catholic Church with those of the Catholic monk Martin Luther, who believed that the Catholic Church had become too powerful, Gustav seized the church's property and diverted its money to the national treasury. In 1527, Lutheranism (a form of Protestantism originated by Martin Luther and his followers) was established as the state religion of Sweden.

ECONOMY

Sweden experienced a rapid cultural development in the 1700s because of its contact with France. Overseas trading increased for a time and resulted in economic security for the Scandinavian country. Then the Napoleonic Wars, which were waged by France against other European countries, had a harsh impact on Sweden. Trade decreased and caused an economic crisis. Even by the late 1700s, Sweden was a poor country, with 90 percent of its population dependent on farming to survive.

After 1800, Sweden's population increased rapidly. The country had not lost lives in battle since early in the century. Smallpox, once the country's deadliest disease, was brought under control by a vaccine. And the introduction of potatoes into Sweden in the late eighteenth century provided a new, affordable source of nutrition. With more people living longer lives, overpopulation threatened the country.

THE CLASS SYSTEM AND POVERTY

Unfortunately, the structure of Sweden's government and state church added to the country's woes. While the formation of the Riksdag in the mid 1400s had spread governing power beyond the king, it enforced a class system that kept the poor powerless. By the mid 1800s, only 5 percent of Sweden's citizens were able to vote in elections. The nobility had access to power simply because they were born into certain families. The gentry had privileges because they owned large pieces of land handed down by their ancestors. The clergy and government officials were considered better than the peasant class, and the small farmers and peasants were treated with more respect than farm workers and landless renters.

This system of class distinctions kept the wealthy and privileged in power and the poor disadvantaged. Sweden's lower classes grew increasingly resentful of the establishment that prevented them from being successful no matter how hard they worked.

Military conscription, which is enforced military service, for Sweden's males was one example of the injustice of the class system. At 20 years of age, each man had to spend three months a year for three years in Sweden's army camps. The training and discipline were harsh. Often the men of privilege and money were able to get out of this duty, whereas the poor had no choice.

The Church of Sweden, rather than being a refuge for the disadvantaged, was part of the mechanism that held them down. Each child born in Sweden became a member of the Lutheran Church at birth and was required to remain a tax-paying member until death. Many clergymen led their flocks as dictators rather than spiritual guides. They taxed parishioners heavily and used the money for their own purposes. Many members of the clergy owned stills that converted grain and potatoes into liquor. The clergy and other landowners who sold this liquor profited, while the widespread abuse of alcohol in Sweden increased.

The lives of the poor were further burdened because only 10 percent of Sweden's land was good for farming. The country became increasingly less able to produce enough food to sustain its citizens. A typical tenant farmer might have lived on land that was owned by the church. He and his family probably lived in a cottage made of timber with a roof made of sod and bark. His children were also obligated to work for the landowner in tending to the live-stock and fieldwork.

People of the middle or lower classes had little chance to buy land. When any land did come up for sale, it was priced out of reach for the struggling classes. Sweden's rural districts became overpopulated, so the market dic-tated very low wages for farm laborers. At the same time, taxes were high on personal property and on land. To add to this misery, there were not enough jobs for those who wanted to work.

Most other European countries had adapted to the Industrial Revolution of the mid-eighteenth century, but Sweden had been slow to transition from an agricultural economy to an industrialized one. Eighty percent of Sweden's

Tracing Your Roots

If you are interested in doing a genealogical search of your family history, there are books, organizations, and websites available to help you. To begin your search, clarify your family name. For descendants of Scandinavians, especially, this may not be an easy task. These countries adhered to the "patronymics" custom, which meant that children used modified versions of their father's first name. In Sweden, the daughters of "Jens" would take on the last name of "Jensdotter," and his sons would take on the last name of "Jensson." To further complicate matters, only a small number of common names existed, so often thousands of "Erik Jenssons" likely lived in the same general time period. Not until the early twentieth century did this system cease. It is helpful to note that Scandinavian women were typically listed under their maiden names and that many Scandinavians Americanized their names after immigrating to America.

Once you've determined your family name, write down your first name and the date and place you were born. It also is helpful to note everything you know about your family history. Be sure to note the sources of this information as specifically as possible. Include your sources' full names, their relationship to you, and where they lived.

As you begin to research, list names, places, and dates or historical periods such as "between World War I and World War II." Then decide how much of your family tree you want to trace. Will you begin with your mother's or your father's side? How far back would you like to research?

To track down information, check the public library for military discharge papers, burial records, and employment records. Look through the government pages of the telephone book for Vital Record Units. Create files and organize them as you collect data.

You may choose to visit Sweden to track down relatives. It may also be helpful to contact the Swedish genealogical organizations listed in the Organizations section at the back of this book. You can write to these organizations for genealogical information. Check your family Bible because it may contain a list of significant family events, dates of birth, and relatives' names. Family scrapbooks, old photos, and high school yearbooks may also yield helpful information. If your family has an old steamer trunk in the basement or attic, it may contain old letters and/or postcards that bear dated stamps.

labor force still depended on farming by 1848. This scenario, together with overpopulation, led to living conditions that were devastating and life threatening, especially to Sweden's lower classes. By the late 1860s, Sweden launched a propaganda campaign to encourage its citizens to leave. Immigration to America became an option for those who feared further poverty and the social implications that went with it.

3

AMERICA FEVER

On Pentecost, we had a really severe storm. . . . We laid in our bunks but the ship's rolling was so strong that several were tossed onto the floor. An old, strict and fat man had his bunk next to ours. Now he laid on his elbows and knees with his broad rear on high, moaned to himself and begged, "Lord God, now it is finished. Oh, Lord, help. Now! Now! Or it is past for all of us." The old man's position and terror was so baroquely comical that I could not restrain myself and broke out in a loud laugh. It affected the other boys so that they [also] joined in, laughing at the poor fellow. But now he became quite brave [through anger] especially towards me who was such a hardened sinner that I could laugh when death was so near.

Trued Granville Persson, 1893

The Homestead Act of 1862 granted full ownership of land to anyone who lived on and farmed a piece of land for five years. The resulting land grab attracted many Swedes, who hoped to establish farms in America's fertile western lands. The immigrants' journey west was often difficult and meant that a family had to live in a covered wagon for months.

While the Swedish people despaired within political, social, and economic systems that were fraught with unfairness, a new country, built upon the ideals of freedom and justice for all, beckoned to them. America, just in its infancy compared with Sweden, was being shaped by immigrants from other countries who had fled from their homelands' own forms of oppression. America offered opportunity and hope for a better life.

In the middle of the 1800s, thousands of emigrants began to leave Sweden. Awaiting them across the Atlantic was a seemingly limitless supply of affordable, fertile land. The Swedes firmly believed that land ownership meant not only a higher standard of living, but a better standing in society as well.

OPPORTUNITIES IN AMERICA
Free Land

The American government, eager to establish settlements across its frontiers, issued two pieces of legislation that set the stage. This legislation was to attract workers to settle the frontier. In 1841, the Preemption Law stated that government-owned land would sell for $1.25 an acre, a bargain even then. This legislation coincided with the beginning of Sweden's group emigration. Then, in 1862, the Homestead Act promised 160 acres of free land to any adult American citizen and to any immigrant who informed the government of his intent to become a U.S. citizen. This one-time offer allowed full ownership to those who lived and farmed the land for five years. Not surprisingly, soon after this legislation was enacted, mass emigration from Sweden began.

From the 1860s to the 1890s, the immigrants' main goal was to own their own farmland. This goal was possible because of the plentitude of jobs available in America. Typically, the homesteader had to invest about $1,000 before his produce could sustain his entire family. There were provisions in the Homestead Act that allowed the homesteaders to take jobs away from their land for up to six months for each of the first five years. Often, these homesteaders would work as railway employees, miners, or lumberjacks during the falls and winters. The money earned during these months would help the immigrants establish themselves financially.

The free government land was not attractive to all immigrants. It was typically located in remote, untamed regions. Those Swedes who came to America with money from the sale of their farm and property in Sweden could afford to buy private land in already established areas.

Gold

In 1848, news of the California Gold Rush caused excitement not just in America, but in Sweden, too. For some poor Swedes, the opportunity to reverse their fortunes must have been irresistible. One Swede, who belonged to a party on their way to the California gold fields in 1859, wrote the following account for the newspaper *Hemlandet* of their trying journey and determination:

> We have a two months' trip before us, making the duration of our entire journey five months. . . . We have forded hundreds of rivers and for five weeks have traversed towering mountains. Our poor oxen are tired out and lean. . . . In order to lighten the load for the oxen we have walked the entire distance and we will have to do likewise on the road to California.

Jobs and Higher Wages

Because America was so new, there was ample opportunity for the Swedes in America to improve their lots more traditionally, too. As Americans were migrating to the West, job opportunities were abundant. In response to an increasing demand for fabric and food, farmers needed hired hands. The construction of railroads, ships, bridges, businesses, homes, and stores required building materials that provided jobs to those willing to work. Workers were also needed to staff the factories, mines, and mills. So even immigrants who arrived with nothing were able to secure employment and save enough money to buy land.

During the mass emigration era in the late 1800s, unemployment was not a great threat in Sweden. The immigrants in this time period were pulled to America not as much by the prospect of the jobs themselves, but by higher wages. The immigrants who settled in the midwestern United States discovered an enormous need for unskilled workers. This need pushed wage levels two to three times higher per year than an unskilled laborer could earn in Sweden. Skilled laborers such as blacksmiths and carpenters could earn even more.

Religious Community

Beyond just economic opportunities, many Swedes were drawn to America to escape the religious oppression of their state church. Sweden's 1726 Conventicle Act ruled that all religious meetings were illegal except those approved by the state church. Even the repeal of this act in 1858 was not enough for many Swedes. Many emigrants disliked the church's subordination to the state. They argued that the church remained more concerned about secular issues than spiritual ones. The revivalist movement that was sweeping across America intrigued these seekers. They were drawn to the possibility of belonging to a community of committed believers.

In Sweden, some spiritual leaders risked penalties of the law to disavow the state church. They formed followings of people and preached their own unique message of salvation. In 1845, one of these leaders, Erik Jansson, was brought to trial for heresy. His crime consisted of leaving the state church, denouncing its leaders, burning books written by Martin Luther, and forbidding his followers to remain in the church. Upon his release from jail, Jansson decided to journey to America. Besides those followers of Erik Jansson, the Janssonists, the Mormons also left Sweden in large numbers.

Fairer Social Structure

America also offered the immigrants a new political and social structure. Until 1866, Sweden was governed by one interpretation of the Riksdag that represented the needs and

Reflections on the Mass Emigration

The following excerpted text was published in the *Korsbaneret* (*The Banner of the Cross*), an annual published by the Lutheran Augustana Book Concern, in 1901. The author reflects on the appeal of America to Swedish immigrants, and wonders if the significant migration to the United States can be connected to God's greater plan.

What can this people's movement mean? It is perhaps yet too early to bother to seek with this question, for God's large world plan was not revealed all at once; since it did not lie on the surface. In due course of time, one can see the result of God's world reign being made manifest. One can well say the space was too crowded in the old world, the bread was scanty, and unskilled laboring people's burdens were too heavy to bear. In America there was ample space, better opportunity to secure a home and it was easier to subsist here than in the old world. There was freedom and lighter burdens to carry oneself here. Surely as this assertion can be, so is it nevertheless God who has definitely set times and boundaries for people to live. Acts 17:26 says, "By one single person he has created everyone. He has allowed them to live over the whole earth and He has confirmed definite times for them and their boundaries within which they will live." This makes us understand that there exists a deeper cause for the general migration; even the mere tangible assets. When one thinks about America's geography, its resources, the thinning out of the earth's people who have been gathered, and the valid constitution, one wishes to know God's design for this country and its people. Does He desire that a plague or scourge were inflicted on us and that we would be the corrector of all the other earth's people? Has He out given us in order to spare us from some ordinary catastrophe, which will cross other parts of the world? Or has He singled us out here in order to especially punish us to warn other peoples and nations? Maybe He will make it clear how people in their own wisdom think; thereby making futility of all human habitation. Yes, who can imagine beforehand how to answer this sort of question. Certainly He has some significant purpose with this country.

Translated from the original Swedish by Judith Gustafson

preferences of the elite. This system caused much friction between the classes. The poorer classes harbored resentment toward the wealthier citizens who controlled much of their lives. Even after the Parliament Act of 1866, which established a bicameral government (government with two legislative branches) in Sweden, the lower classes were without a political voice.

In America, by contrast, there was no royalty. There were no noblemen or gentry whose living depended on the high taxation of the lower classes. Young men from the poorer classes were not subjected to a military duty from which the rich could escape. The American government did not force its citizens to pay taxes to support clergymen whose loyalties were aligned with the wealthy rather than with the needy. And the right to vote and take part in the local government did not depend on ownership of land.

When the American Civil War broke out in 1861, the United States Consul in Stockholm claimed that thousands of Swedes and Norwegians were determined to join the Union Army. Although many of these men likely volunteered as a quick way to get to America, the willingness of many Scandinavians to fight with the North was based on their rejection of slavery. They viewed slavery as an extreme form of serfdom.

American railroad and steamship companies recognized the potential to make money on the transportation of immigrants. Both industries saturated the Scandinavian countries with propaganda about the better life awaiting them in America. They also advertised in European newspapers and published their own. They even hired agents to promote the New World to friends and family still in Sweden. Typically, these agents were immigrants who had already transitioned successfully to life in America. Some were stationed in America, others in Sweden. One to two agents were assigned to each church in central and southern Sweden. Typical agents included hotel and inn keepers, railroad and postal employees, as well as

EMIGRATION

UP THE MISSISSIPPI RIVER.

The attention of Emigrants and the Public generally, is called to the now rapidly improving

TERRITORY OF MINNESOTA,

Containing a population of 150,000, and goes into the Union as a State during the present year. According to an act of Congress passed last February, the State is munificently endowed with Lands for Public Schools and State Universities, also granting five per cent. on all sales of U. S. Lands for Internal Improvements. On the 3d March, 1857, grants of Land from Congress was made to the leading Trunk Railroads in Minnesota, so that in a short time the trip from New Orleans to any part of the State will be made in from two and a half to three days. The

CITY OF NININGER,

Situated on the Mississippi River, 35 miles below St. Paul, is now a prominent point for a large Commercial Town, being backed by an extensive Agricultural, Grazing and Farming Country; has fine streams in the interior, well adapted for Milling in all its branches; and Manufacturing **WATER POWER** to any extent.

Mr. JOHN NININGER, (a Gentleman of large means, ideas and liberality, speaking the various languages), is the principal Proprietor of **Nininger**. He laid it out on such principles as to encourage all **MECHANICS**, Merchants, or Professions of all kinds, on the same equality and footing; the consequence is, the place has gone ahead with such rapidity that it is now an established City, and will annually double in population for years to come.

Persons arriving by Ship or otherwise, can be transferred without expense to Steamers going to Saint Louis; or stop at Cairo, and take Railroad to Dunleith (on the Mississippi). Steamboats leave Saint Louis and Dunleith daily for **NININGER**, and make the trip from Dunleith in 36 to 48 hours.

NOTICES.

1. All Railroads and Steamboats giving this card a conspicuous place, or *gratuitous insertion* in their cards, **AIDS THE EMIGRANT** and forwards their own interest.

2. For authentic documents, reliable information, and all particulars in regard to Occupations, Wages, Preëmpting Lands (in neighborhood), Lumber, Price of Lots, Expenses, &c., apply to

THOMAS B. WINSTON, 27 Camp street, New Orleans.
ROBERT CAMPBELL, St. Louis.
JOSEPH B. FORBES, Dunleith.

American steamship and railroad companies recognized the money-making opportunities provided by waves of immigration. Handbills like this one promoted settlement in towns like Nininger, Minnesota, and of course encouraged railway and steamship travel as a way to get there.

merchants. Some received commission for every emigrant they persuaded to relocate. Many earned free passage back to Sweden.

Even more effective than the transportation industry's propaganda were visits and "America letters" (letters sent to Sweden about life in America) from Swedish emigrants. When a letter from America reached Sweden, it was read aloud to entire communities. Sometimes these letters were passed among members of a parish. The letters were often printed in Swedish newspapers and convinced even more Swedes to sail to America. Gustaf Unonius, who emigrated in 1841 and called himself "the first emigrant," authored many America letters that were printed in a Stockholm newspaper. In one such correspondence, Unonius declared that in America "no epithets of degradation are applied to men of humble toil." This remark likely made a strong and positive impression on the lower-class Swedes, who had toiled for decades under degrading and humbling conditions. The combination of the transportation industry's propaganda campaign and the America letters sparked what was referred to as "America Fever."

THE THREE WAVES OF EMIGRATION

The general characteristics of the emigrants and what motivated them to leave Sweden varied. In his book, *Letters from the Promised Land,* H. Arnold Barton groups the emigrants into three major waves. The first wave includes those who left Sweden between 1840 and 1864. The second wave includes those who emigrated between 1865 and 1889, and the third wave included those who departed between 1890 and 1914.

Emigrants who left early in the first wave were typically unable to purchase land in Sweden. Neither rich nor poor, they appreciated that they could have access to the land ownership that America offered. These emigrants were fueled by the need for economic security. Many emigrants early in this first wave were also seeking an escape from the tyranny of the state church and the freedom to worship in their own way. The

California Gold Rush in the late 1840s inspired still other emigrants. There were also plenty of Swedes who were eager to take advantage of the 1862 Homestead Act's offer of free land.

The end of the American Civil War in 1865 signaled a rebirth in immigration to America. Those emigrants in the second wave were escaping the hunger that resulted from three consecutive years of crop failure between 1867 and 1869. In the late 1870s, Swedes faced another agricultural crisis, when wheat from Australia, Argentina, and North America caused Swedish-grown cereal prices to decrease sharply. With this added economic hardship, more emigrants departed for America. In the 1880s, Swedish emigration increased dramatically. Many Swedish men set out to work in Michigan iron mines. Increasing numbers settled in Chicago, Minneapolis, and St. Paul, where they could find jobs. Swedish girls emigrated for jobs as maids with middle-class American families.

During this time, transportation became more affordable, faster, and more comfortable. While competition in the transportation industry reduced costs by more than 50 percent between 1865 and 1890, pay for American farm workers increased by more than one-third. Rather than traveling in groups, many young men and women traveled alone. Often these young adults established themselves, sent part of their earnings home, and eventually bought tickets for family members to join them.

From 1890 until 1914, during the third wave, the number of emigrants leaving Sweden fluctuated more than ever in reaction to events taking place in both Sweden and America. In 1892, when military conscription increased to 90 days a year, many Swedish men sought refuge in America. The Klondike Gold Rush in the late 1800s drew large numbers of Swedes to the Yukon Territory and Alaska. The year 1901 marked an increase in emigration from the year before, likely because military conscription was increased again. The poorer Swedes especially resented this imposition. In 1904, the Swedish government drafted two bills that were to restrict emigration. From 1907 until 1909, strikes, lockouts, and labor unrest rocked Sweden, and, again, new waves of emigration resulted. By 1911, over 50 percent of Swedish emigrants were city-dwelling, industrial workers. When the Swedish government implemented reforms in 1914 in response to the grievances of the poorer classes, emigration to America slowed. The coming of World War I around this same time added to the downturn in emigration rates.

OBSTACLES TO EMIGRATION

Despite many Swedes' determination to emigrate, the obstacles to leaving their homeland were numerous. During certain periods in the country's history, the government restricted people from leaving. In the early 1840s, one of these restrictions was lifted and opened the floodgates of emigration. Another obstacle for the emigrants was the lack of financial resources. After all, poverty is what drove many to leave their homeland in the first place. Those who could scrape together the $12 or $13 cargo ship fare for each family member would then need to gather enough food to feed their family for the seven- to ten-week trip. During the early years of emigration, the ship's company did not provide passenger meals.

Assuming a Swedish citizen had the financial means to sail to America, he then had to face the parish clergy to receive certification of his good standing in the community. An early emigrant from Ostergotland recalled the kind of confrontation that typically ensued:

> And then this most weighty document had to be presented to the Governor of the province in order to receive a passport from that august personage and to do this was a serious affair as a person heard nothing but jeers and insults from the time one entered the anteroom and gave his name and business to the liveried flunky, until he got outside again of the executive mansion.

One emigrant recalled the parish pastor cautioning his father about the dangers of crossing the ocean. He warned of "ferocious beasts, blood-thirsty Indians and those Americans who were a people without religion or morality of any kind whatever."

For many Swedes who planned a better life in America, perhaps the greatest obstacle to leaving was the knowledge that they might never again see the people and things they had known all their lives.

ROUGH VOYAGES TO AMERICA

In the mid 1800s, when significant numbers of Swedes began to voyage across the Atlantic, the emigrants typically found themselves passengers aboard cargo ships. Not all these ships were seaworthy, and most were unclean. Passengers took turns cooking their food on brick-and-mortar-lined barrels that had iron bars across the surface. Salt water was in plentiful supply for bathing and washing clothes.

Disease ran rampant among the passengers who were crowded into primitive sleeping and living quarters below deck. Double-stacked bunks lined both sides along the length of the ship, and four to five people shared one bunk. The air below deck reeked of body odors, the smell of oil from lamps, and, in stormy weather, the stench of vomit from seasick passengers also hung in the buttoned down quarters.

By 1859, steamships carrying Swedish passengers typically served porridge, dried fruit, pea soup, rice and molasses, fish, beef, and pork. Passengers were also offered biscuits, butter, tea, and coffee. Emigrant Maria Helene Jonsdotter sent a letter to her sister in Sweden advising her to "not take a lot of linen cloth. Instead bring plenty of tinware. Pack some food so that you have something to eat in case you cannot stomach what they give you at sea. Hardtack is good; also some cheese and dried meat. Take along a food basket." Emigrants also packed clothes, household goods, and tools.

In the late 1800s, Ellis Island in New York Harbor became the central point of entry for thousands of European immigrants, including many Swedes. Here, immigrants had to be registered, processed, and examined by a doctor before they could officially set foot on American soil.

By 1865, steamships typically picked up Swedish travelers in Gothenburg. From there, they traveled to Hull, England. Emigrants would then take the train from Hull to Liverpool. A few days later, they would depart Liverpool and take a ship to New York, Québec, or Boston.

Emigrants experienced terrible seasickness on their journey to America. One emigrant, Andrew Peterson, described how "in the evening most of the passengers were stricken by sea-sickness, to the extent there was terrible vomiting along the railing." Peterson also described a more tragic scene that was, unfortunately, too common to the early emigrants:

> Gustaf's youngest daughter . . . died at six o'clock in the morning at the age of one year and five months. The body was wrapped in a sheet, then it was wound about with a sail, with a sinker around the feet. Next it was carried up on deck and laid on a plank that was placed on the railing. Then the captain read the funeral service over it, and it was lowered deep into the deep grave, about thirty-four fathoms [204 feet] deep . . .

By 1855, those emigrants who survived the Atlantic voyage landed in Castle Garden at the eastern edge of Manhattan Island. This first landing station accepted immigrants for most of the 1800s. Here, the immigrants went through customs and immigration control. The immigrants could usually locate an interpreter here, who could guide them through the regulated process and provide them with tips regarding lodging and transportation to their ultimate destination.

When the federal government gained control of the immigration process in the late 1800s, they moved their headquarters to Ellis Island in New York Harbor. This new point of entry would welcome thousands more Swedish immigrants in the years to come.

4

TAMERS
OF THE
FRONTIER

As the sun was rising we passed through the long but beautiful harbor's rocky entrance, beautiful in the dawn of morning. Shortly after the steamship anchored in the harbor we were able to land in the [Castle Garden] where we separated into groups to orderly pass some "profound old men" who sat at their desks and good-naturedly questioned us as we reached them. They checked our tickets, money, etc. Then it was [time] to go down to another area where our baggage went through Customs examination. The Customs attendants seemed to think themselves important and didn't bother themselves much to check our boxes and suitcases. Going through Customs was much easier than I expected. Our tickets and baggage were all cleared by 5 P.M. so we were free then to board our train.

Esaias J. Stolpe, October 1901

Prior to the establishment of Ellis Island, immigrants to America who came through New York Harbor were processed at Manhattan's Castle Garden. In spite of the high price of passage, which could easily cost a family its entire life's savings, the conditions for passage were less than luxurious, with overcrowding and unsanitary conditions standard fare.

FROM THE LANDING STATION WESTWARD

Especially in the mid to late 1800s, the immigrants' first impression of America was clouded by the harsh realities that awaited them upon landing. A Swedish clergyman described the scene he witnessed at Castle Garden in 1865:

The Swedish immigrant Olaf Krans created this painting of the Swedish settlement at Bishop Hill, Illinois. Established by Erik Jansson in 1846, the settlement struggled before achieving prosperity. Ten miles away, in the village of Andover, the Reverend Lars P. Esbjorn established the first Swedish Lutheran Church in the Midwest.

opportunities. M. F. Hokanson, a blacksmith by trade, became their pastor.

Within 10 miles of Bishop Hill, the Reverend Lars P. Esbjorn, a Lutheran pastor from Sweden, established the first Swedish Lutheran Church in the Midwest in the village of Andover, Illinois. Pastors Esbjorn and Hokanson's spiritual influence eventually resulted in the formation of the Augustana Lutheran Synod in America.

CHICAGO SETTLEMENT

Other Swedish immigrants in this first wave crowded into Chicago. In the 1840s and 1850s, they lived in slums along the Chicago River. By 1852, poor living conditions among the immigrants caused an epidemic of cholera.

Large numbers of Swedes continued to settle in Illinois throughout the second wave. By the 1860s, the immigrants moved north and built homes around Chicago Avenue, which became known as Swedish Farmers' Street. Many held steady employment in low-paying jobs. The United States census in 1880 showed that the largest population of Swedish immigrants had settled in Illinois. By 1884, almost 10,000 Swedes were living in Chicago, and a part of the city became known as Swede Town. By the end of the nineteenth century, Swede Town began deteriorating, and those who could afford to moved to the suburbs of Hyde Park, Englewood, and Lake View.

MINNESOTA SETTLEMENT

Around 1890, the beginning of the third wave of immigration, Minnesota took the lead as the home to the largest number of Swedish immigrants. It became known as the Swedish State. Between 12 and 13 percent of the state's population were Swedish Americans. By this time, the largest ethnic group in Minnesota was Scandinavians. Although parts of Minnesota bore a strong resemblance to Sweden's topography, most immigrants did not base their decision to live there on that fact. The Swedish actually ended up in the state in such large numbers because Minnesota happened to be the land available to them as the American frontier expanded.

RURAL AND URBAN SWEDISH SETTLEMENTS

By 1910, 45 percent of Swedish Americans were located in the north-central part of the United States. At the same time, increasing numbers of Swedes were settling in the Rocky

Mountain states, in the forested regions of the Northwest, and in California. Swedish immigrants who had skills in industry were moving to New York and Massachusetts.

Swedish Americans lived in predominantly rural areas during the 1880s, but by 1910 at least 60 percent lived in urban areas. This was typical of American society's process of urbanization.

Typically, the immigrants who had lived in rural Swedish districts tended to relocate to agricultural states like Kansas and Iowa. Those from industrial districts in Sweden tended to relocate to places such as Pennsylvania and Massachusetts, which were centers of manufacturing. Farmers from certain rural Swedish districts set up their new homes on the midwestern prairies. And the forested areas of the northern United States and Canada became home to Swedes who had worked in Swedish sawmills.

After 1900, the revitalization of the Industrial Revolution increased the need for workers in urban areas. This resulted in increasing numbers of rural immigrants settling in the industrialized cities of the United States.

Collectively, the Swedish immigrants made an impact on and took part in shaping their new homeland. By taking advantage of the affordable land offered by the railroad companies and the U.S. government, they helped tame the American frontier. Ultimately, Sweden also supplied some of the labor needed to sustain the Industrial Revolution that transitioned the country from a primarily rural society to an industrial one. Swedish immigrants worked in mines, built railroads, cleared land, and produced lumber as the country expanded westward.

By 1860, more than 50 percent of the world's railroad tracks were in the United States. The wealthy railroad businessman, James J. Hill, once declared, "Give me Swedes, snuff, and whiskey, and I'll build a railroad to Hell." This improved transportation system helped create a market in which goods could be traded and sold across the nation.

SWEDES' PART IN AMERICAN CIVIL WAR

When the American Civil War broke out in 1861, Swedish Americans stood behind President Lincoln. Over 3,000 Swedish immigrants served in the Union Army, the greatest number coming from Illinois and Minnesota. One of these men, Hans Mattson, appealed to his fellow Scandinavian-American citizens, "Countrymen, arise to arms; our adopted country calls! Let us prove ourselves worthy of that land, and of those heroes from whom we descend." Mattson and other Swedish men formed Company D of the Third Minnesota Regiment. Twelve Swedish-American Union Army colonels and three brigadier generals helped to lead the North to victory. Approximately 25 Swedish Americans joined the Confederate Army.

John Ericsson, another Swedish American, played a vital role in the North's ultimate success. Using his experience from designing defense ships in Sweden, he drafted plans for a 600-ton navy frigate named the *Princeton* in 1861. This Union ship was unique in that it was made of iron instead of wood and was driven by propeller. The next year he designed the *Monitor*, which became his best-known ship. Thousands of people traveled to the Virginia shore to watch the *Monitor* battle the *Merrimack*, the South's battleship. Although neither side won the four-hour duel, naval combat would never be the same.

MORE HARDSHIPS

Even the Swedish immigrants who arrived after the end of the Civil War in 1865 faced considerable challenges. Although the immigrants likely had the luxury of an interpreter while being processed at Castle Garden, after that point they had to fend for themselves using a language that few Americans understood.

Other challenges faced by the Swedish Americans were the economic hardships that many immigrants fled from in Sweden and arrived to once in America. After their limited supply of food from Sweden was gone, they had little, if any, money to buy more. Growing their own food would not be possible until months after the immigrants purchased and cleared land for planting. Their rustic homes were furnished with makeshift furniture; their wooden chests from home became their kitchen tables. Wooden planks served as beds.

Those who settled in wooded areas faced the laborious challenge of clearing land for farming and for building homes. Those who settled on the prairie did not face this issue but instead had to make homes of available materials, since lumber was in short supply. Often these homes were made of sod.

Prairie life was lonely and harsh. Frigid cold and blinding snowstorms made winters treacherous. Summers could be just as difficult because of scorching temperatures, prairie fires, hailstorms, and grasshopper invasions that often ruined entire fields of crops. Women especially found life on the prairie difficult. The nearest neighbor likely lived miles away. Churches and schools did not exist on the prairie during the early years of Swedish immigration. Women were often left alone with the children while their husbands were away on business. Isolated, they sometimes had to deal with the loss of sick children who could not survive without a doctor's aid.

THE SWEDES AND THE SIOUX

The Swedish immigrants who had settled in Minnesota had learned for the most part to coexist with the Native Americans who shared the land with them. One Swedish immigrant recalled that:

When we got located on our long-sought-after land, we found ourselves surrounded by Indians. We treated them in the most friendly manner, being careful not to show fear, nor did we in any way antagonize them. We traded with them, receiving venison in exchange for bread and potatoes. They did us no

While the Homestead Act made land easily available, settling and farming it was hard. Lumber was scarce on the prairie, forcing many Swedish immigrants like those here to build and live in sod houses. Harsh winters, brush fires, hailstorms, and swarms of grasshoppers further challenged the resolve of these new immigrants.

harm, though we were sometimes startled by their uncivilized habit of covering our windows with their blankets while they peered in on us. We were just as much of a curiosity to them as their painted faces and strange ways were to us.

In 1862, as more and more white settlers filled the Minnesota Valley, the Sioux Indians grew anxious. They knew white settlers had taken land from the Native Americans in the East. The Sioux, realizing that most army troops were away fighting the Civil War, decided to take action and

My America

Emil Granfelt, from Smaland, Sweden
An Account of Life as a Klondike Gold Miner
Alaska and the Yukon Territory, 1900

My cabin is ten feet long and eight feet wide. The window is a little hold in the log wall. The door opening faces the east and measures four and a half by three feet. When the wind blows the door is closed, for a piece of sailcloth has to serve in place of a walnut panel. The roof consists of poles caulked with moss and bark. Half the cabin is my bedroom, but when it rains I must rig up an awning over my bed to keep from getting soaked through. . . . Through the window and the cracks I have not filled with moss the flies have entry. The floor in that part of the cabin not taken up by my bed consists of the same material Adam had in paradise. . . .

My greatest enemies are the mosquitoes and a bird called the Alaska bluebird. The former swarm around me day and night, and the bird begins shrieking and carrying on every morning at half past three. But my revolver has sent many of them back to their maker. . . .

On 4 July I was in Eagle City. It was Independence Day and it was celebrated as usual in town with a salute. Fifty cannon shots were fired by Uncle Sam's soldiers.

Later there were all kinds of sports. The Indians took part in a competition that was very funny to watch. Some ten or fifteen Indians competed to see who could get across the river first, with some small, light birch-bark canoes. They paddled with such speed that their black hair stood straight out behind them. A competition which only Indians took part in was to jump on a hide stretched out by many other Indians. Whoever was able to jump highest won the competition. A hunch-backed Indian boy took first prize. Later there were many competitions which only the whites took part in.

A whole lot of Indians with women and children had come into town. They belonged to a tribe with three or four hundred members which lived two English miles from Eagle City. Many of them spoke good English. . . .

Next day I went up to my mine. I then had along with me a large load of provisions. Then I worked in the mine until 23 July, then I left my work to go down to Dawson. . . .

protect what was theirs. Little Crow, a Sioux Indian, led his tribe in a series of attacks against the settlers.

In the end, hundreds of immigrant houses were burned to the ground, and many immigrants and Native Americans lost their lives. The bloody uprisings were only a temporary obstacle for the immigrants, however, as many ravaged settlements were rebuilt within months.

Despite such hardships, most Swedish Americans appreciated what their new home offered them. A Minnesota pastor wrote home to Sweden in the mid 1800s:

> Say what you will about America, one thing is certain, and that is that those who wish to and can work can escape from want; for work and earnings for both men and women are not lacking here. The Swedes in this area are not prosperous; but this is not to be wondered at; for when they came a few years ago, there was complete wilderness here and you surely know that new land cannot be broken, fenced, and made into fertile fields quickly, nor buildings put up for themselves and their livestock; and therefore it is not surprising that we still have very poor houses and that things are far from what we would wish; but they get better each year . . .

5 SOCIAL ISSUES IN INDUSTRIAL AMERICA

We arrived in New York without a penny, and . . . there was no employment in sight. But then a Swedish gentleman put in his appearance and offered us employment. . . . Instead of keeping his promise he brought us to the southern states. . . . In New York he had promised that food, lodging, bedclothes, and a physician's services would be furnished free of cost in addition to monthly wages of thirteen dollars for myself and eight dollars for my wife. But instead I received ten dollars and my wife two. We are twelve Swedes, including men, women, and children, and receive less than twelve cans of buttermilk per day, cornmeal for pancakes in place of bread, and a small amount of pork. This is our daily allowance. We work hard all day, at night sleep on a hard brick floor, and an hour before sunrise begin work.

Olof Brink, Virginia, 1865

The scarcity of lumber challenged Swedish immigrants to build their homes from available materials. Sod houses like this one, made from dried and stacked strips of grassy earth, were common. A wagon cover often served as a roof.

Even though eagerly awaited, the Swedish immigrants' arrival at their final destinations did not signal the end of their struggles. The first year in particular was difficult for the Swedish immigrants in the first wave. Aware of the severe winters in their adopted land, these pioneers made every effort to arrive at their final destinations before winter did.

BUILDING A HOME

Some Swedish pioneers met up with family or friends from Sweden and lived with them temporarily. Those who did not have this luxury would construct makeshift homes from available materials. For some, their new home was a tent, for others a shanty. Many Swedes were carpenters and skilled at building log homes. Their goal was to eventually build log homes when the weather and their resources permitted.

On the prairie, where trees were scarce, the immigrants' homes were made of strips of sod. These strips were dried and stacked like bricks to form houses called "soddies." Other times, the prairie pioneers dug their homes into the side of a hill. A wagon cover or tree branches and tall prairie grass served as the roof. A hole was left open in the roof to vent smoke. The only opening that allowed sunlight in was the door; consequently these homes were like caves. One young immigrant described her first experience staying in the "home of my Aunt Hannah and Uncle Hakan Nelson. A dug out in the hill—we slept upstairs. I remember snakes hanging in the roof . . ."

The pioneers who lived far from streams or lakes had to dig their own wells with whatever tools were available. The wooden chests brought from Sweden served as their tables or chairs. Their pillows were stuffed with cattail down. Buffalo chips, which were dried buffalo waste, served as fuel until the buffalo were killed off. Prairie grass then filled this need.

Before winter arrived, the Swedish-American men typically left their wives and families to find work with the lumber companies or the railroad. While her husband earned much needed money during his months away, the pioneer's wife was left to care for their homestead and children. Children helped with farming and household chores as soon as they were physically able. One young Swedish American named Einar explained:

While Father was sick, I had to start doing fieldwork—I was only thirteen. I stood on a box and harnessed the horses. I seeded eleven acres of wheat north of the place; I had to walk behind the drill and couldn't see above it but had to look between the shoes. . . . After I had seeded, I had to drag, then I used four horses. There came up a dust storm, my cap blew off and scared the horses so they had a runaway ... Helga came out to help me—she was crying. We got the horses unhooked and apart and straightened out. They didn't get hurt but I didn't do any more fieldwork that day.

Sometimes to ease the burden of those first most difficult years on the frontier, a few families would group together to form a farm community. They worked on a collaborative basis to build log homes, to clear the land, and to buy farm equipment. This system allowed for at least one male to stay with the women and children while the others were away earning money for the group.

Many immigrants sent letters back to Sweden about the marvels of America's untamed beauty, but most were unprepared for the harshness of its seasons. The pioneers faced locust plagues, tornadoes, prairie fires, droughts, and floods.

The new immigrants from Sweden were also amazed by the freedom they found in America. They were free of the government that catered to the elite, free from the state church's clergy, and free from a class system they could not rise out of in Sweden. Although the immigrants appreciated the American's casual behavior, they were put off by their crude manners and lack of decorum. They were also bewildered by the lawlessness of American life, such as the political corruption, the murder in the cities, and the Indian massacres and subsequent retaliations.

EMIGRATION CONTINUES

Still, the Swedish immigrants didn't lose sight of the opportunities to better their lives in America. The Swedes in the second wave emigrated just after the American Civil War ended and reaped the benefits of a strong economy in the northern and eastern states. Mass emigration paralleled the demands for skilled and unskilled laborers. Between 1868 and 1873, 125,000 Swedes immigrated to America. Most were farmers who responded to the free land offers that were outlined in the

Homestead Act, but others were shoemakers, tailors, carpenters, and blacksmiths.

Before the start of the third wave of migration in 1890, most Swedish immigrants began their American life in the Midwest. The Midwest drew railroad workers, farm workers, lumberjacks, maids, and unskilled laborers. Others who settled there accepted jobs in factories or in homes in Chicago and Minneapolis. Some immigrants stayed with relatives or friends in the East. The East drew industrial and more highly skilled laborers.

LABOR DISPUTES AND STRIKES

America's industrial growth after the Civil War provided opportunities for the immigrants; however, it came at a price. Many skilled workers were replaced by anyone who could learn to operate a machine. Employers had increasing power over workers, since workers were easily replaced. In the last decades of the nineteenth century, there was great labor discontent and violent strikes. In 1877, a nationwide railroad strike resulted in a virtual halt of all production because materials couldn't be transported across the country. One Swedish-American striker expressed his frustration in *The North American Review*:

Forty years ago my father came over to this country from Sweden. He had a small business and a large family. In Europe business does not grow as fast as children come, and poverty over there is an inheritance. He heard that North America was peopled and governed by working men, and the care of the states was mainly engaged in the welfare and prosperity of labor. That moved him, and so I came to be born here. He, and millions like him, made this country . . . what it is . . . So it was before the war, but since then, it seems to me, the power has got fixed so long in one set of hands [the industrialists'] that things are settling down into a condition like what my father left behind him in Europe forty years ago, and what stands there still. I mean the slavery of labor.

The tendency of the early Swedish immigrants was to establish communities made up of other Swedes they had traveled with across the Atlantic. This was helpful not only because they could preserve their language and customs this way, but because it was economically advantageous as well. The Swedish Americans tended to find the most opportunities for employment in those areas where they were part of the majority population. In those areas where they were outnumbered by early immigrants and native-born Americans,

Domestic Workers

The increasing numbers of males who immigrated to America negatively affected young women in Sweden. The women's prospects for a marriage partner declined, and an excess in the female labor market kept their wages low. Meanwhile in America, the families who could afford it were looking for live-in maids.

From the late 1860s and after, many of the newest Swedish immigrants were young, single women. Because Scandinavian girls were in demand, most had no difficulty securing employment. Rather than feeling degraded by their social standing as servants, they were pleased that they no longer had to do strenuous outdoor work. They had their own bedrooms, regular days off, and weekly pay. They were treated respectfully by the families they served and by American men in general. These were luxuries compared with what they were accustomed to in Sweden. These young Swedish women had the option of leaving their employers for a new position whenever they chose. They picked up the American language and customs more readily than the Swedish men because they were an integral part of American families rather than part of a work group made up of other Swedes.

The Swedish men often resented the luxuries of employment these women enjoyed and their tendency to put on high-class American airs. These domestic workers were strong supporters of the American middle-class society, even after they married their Swedish husbands. After all, this society provided them with the opportunity to rise above their meager beginnings.

While many Swedish men found work as craftsmen or in the mining and railroad industries, young women often served as live-in maids. A maid was given her own room, a weekly wage, and regular days off – luxuries when compared to her life in Sweden.

they found employment opportunities more limited. This was true for farmers as well as laborers.

IMMIGRANTS IN THE MIDWEST AND WEST

Immigrants who arrived in America during the first two waves tamed and developed much of the midwestern frontier, and new immigrants continued to settle there. Although there were still farm and domestic job opportunities for immigrants who arrived in the Midwest after 1890 (the beginning of the third wave), those who wanted to work for the railroad or as lumberjacks had to look farther west for employment. So many

Swedish immigrants would make their living as lumberjacks in the Pacific Northwest that the crosscut saw was dubbed the "Swedish fiddle."

During this third wave of immigration, factories and public service sectors offered work to those Swedish immigrants who were unskilled. Those who had worked in industrial positions in Sweden relocated to the industrial cities in the East.

Even though many Swedes could have found work in their homeland during this time period, they could not have made the kind of money that America offered them. Farm workers in Sweden earned about $.30 a day; those in America could earn a daily wage of up to $4. Industrial wages in America were also considerably higher than those in Sweden.

After 1900, in the middle of the third wave, many Swedish Americans bristled at how the United States treated its industrial workers in contrast to Sweden. Swedish industry was influenced by Europe's more liberal treatment of its employees. As labor-market conditions toughened, many American industries pushed their employees hard for increased production. Cutthroat competition and corruption led to growing hardship for the American workers.

While the first immigrants had to forge their own trails to where they would live and work, those who came later could often depend on the railroad to take them there. By the late 1800s, trains were transporting more passengers across the frontier than the stagecoaches and steamboats combined.

SWEDISH RELIGIOUS ORGANIZATIONS

Most of the Swedish immigrants avoided settling near other ethnic groups who crowded into the cities along the East Coast. They were quick to establish churches that united them to other Swedish Americans in their new homeland and provided them with a place to congregate for worship and socializing. For the first time in their lives, Swedish immigrants were able to worship as they pleased. Some left the Lutheran religion they had been born into. Some who remained Lutheran followed a stricter, more conservative form of religion than they'd grown up with. They were part of the Augustana Synod, which included more Swedish Americans than any other religious sect. The synod grew from 3,000 to over 84,000 members between 1860 and 1890.

Decades earlier, between the late 1840s and early 1850s, the Swedish Methodist Church welcomed fellow Swedes to America in New York City. During this time frame, numerous Swedish Methodist churches began in the East and the Midwest.

Gustav Palmquist, once a schoolteacher in Sweden, established America's first Swedish Baptist Church in Rock Island, Illinois, in 1852. Palmquist had been a convert from the Lutheran religion to the Methodist religion in Sweden. It was during his evangelistic travels in America that he became a Baptist.

While still in Sweden, almost 17,000 Swedes had responded to the evangelistic efforts of the Mormon Church between 1850 and 1909. About 8,000 of those who had adopted the faith immigrated to America.

The Mission Covenant Church that started in the Midwest also claimed Swedish Americans as members. In the 1870s, it joined with other like-minded societies to create the Evangelical Lutheran Mission Synod, which became a national organization. When this synod merged with the Asgar Synod in 1885, they formed the second-largest Swedish-American denomination, the Swedish Evangelical Mission Covenant of America. More than 40,000 members belonged to this church organization by 1930.

These Swedish-American religious organizations strived to not only better their members spiritually, but to better society as well. Their activities involved meeting the immigrants' educational and medical needs. The church established and funded colleges, seminaries, and schools. Hospitals and homes for orphans and the aged were also church sponsored. To spread religious and social news to Swedish Americans,

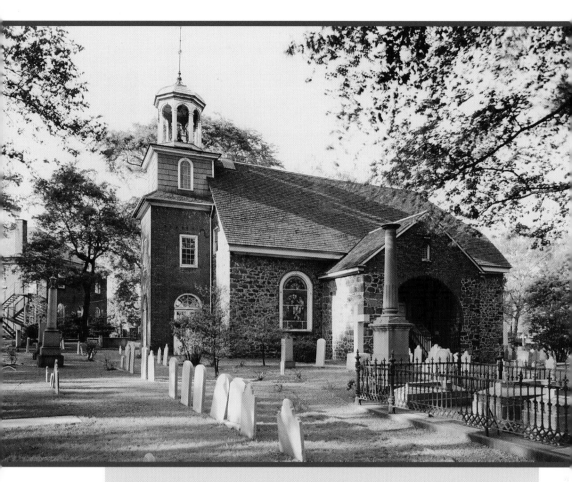

Swedish immigrants were quick to establish new churches or join existing congregations in America. During the 1800s, Swedes were members of various Lutheran, Methodist, Baptist, and Mormon churches throughout the eastern and midwestern United States. This church, established by Swedes in Delaware, was built in 1698.

they also published newspapers, journals, and books. The Augustana Book Concern, an offshoot of the largest Swedish-American synod that was founded in 1884, was one of the most influential publishers of this kind.

For the Swedish immigrants, the traditional Christian concept of accepting their lots in this world was eventually replaced by the secular pursuit of improving their lots materially. Still, these Christians held steadfast to their faith that a better world awaited them and their loved ones in the afterlife.

SWEDISH CLUBS, ORGANIZATIONS, AND CULTURE

Once the Swedish Americans began to settle in and conditions for them normalized, secular organizations were established and flourished. During the 1870s, more than 70 different Swedish societies and clubs existed. The purpose of each organization varied; some were gymnastic clubs, choral groups, and fraternal organizations. Some provided insurance and financial assistance to their members. These organizations illustrated the desire of many Swedish Americans to remain tied to their Swedish culture.

By 1910, the number of Swedish-born Americans was at its peak, and the Swedish-American culture reached an all-time high. Swedish theaters were wildly popular, and more Swedish-American books and periodicals were published than ever before.

SWEDISH SUPPORTERS OF POLITICAL PARTIES

Swedish Americans before 1850 were traditionally supporters of the Democratic Party. Most immigrants, regardless of their nationality, aligned themselves with this party because its platform championed immigrant issues. In the mid 1850s, many Swedish voters were drawn to the newly formed Republican Party. They supported the party's stand against slavery, and they were certainly excited about the party's promise of free land to new settlers. Swedish Americans became some of Abraham Lincoln's staunchest supporters. Their support materialized in a high percentage of Swedish Americans who volunteered to serve in the Union Army. In Illinois alone, more than half of the 2,500 Swedes who qualified to serve in the military enlisted as volunteers.

A. Carlsson Warberg, a Swedish officer who volunteered to

serve in the Union Army, had the honor of attending a White House reception in 1862. His admiration of President Lincoln is evident in his recollection of that event: "Anyone the president did not know was immediately presented by those around him or by the secretary, and since many mistakes were made which were corrected by the person in question, there was unconstrained merriment, which was further heightened by the hearty grin, quip, or short appropriate anecdote which the illustrious host had ready at hand . . . " Even after Lincoln's assassination in 1865, most Swedish Americans continued to idolize him.

Within a couple of decades after Lincoln's death, the increased incomes of Swedish Americans often translated into prepaid tickets sent to relatives still in Sweden. With improved and less expensive transportation, the flow of those who wanted to settle in America continued. Those who immigrated toward the end of and after the nineteenth century had a choice that those before them did not previously have: they could settle in America permanently or return to Sweden.

6 SWEDISH IDENTITY ACROSS THE ATLANTIC

I finally left Chicago and made my way to Pennsylvania where I worked on the railroads for about four years; then I entered into matrimony with a girl from my native place. She had a little money, and I had saved up a little so that we bought a little farm. . . . This farm we kept for two years, then we sold it; we bought another 120 acres for $1,000. . . . Now we worked on this for a couple of years and then there was a sawmill nearby which was for sale and we bought it for $2,000. Now I sawed timber both for myself and for others so that in two years I had paid for the sawmill. . . .

Now I began buying up larger and smaller pieces of land with timber, and that went fine. My old farm sold, a larger and better one bought, a general store started, town properties purchased, and then I started building houses in the towns of Youngsville and Jamestown, New York. So today I have 300 acres of land, a good farm, good sawmill . . . two stores, eight houses in the towns, and ten lease-holders who pay me an annual income of $900. Meanwhile we have brought up eight children, of which some are married. . . . If I had stayed behind in Sweden, I would have been a hired hand, at the very best a crofter.

Response by E. C. S., Pennsylvania, around 1907
to the Swedish government's request for
information as to why people had emigrated

Swedish immigrants relied on Swedish-language newspapers to help preserve their culture, inform their readers, and advertise social and political events. During the late 1800s, over 1,000 different Swedish-American newspapers were published in 30 states.

B y the twentieth century, Swedish immigrants had increasing opportunities to return to their native land. Most immigrants stayed and began to focus on adapting to and finding success in America.

SWEDISH AMERICANS MOVE INTO POLITICS

While most Swedish Americans had strongly supported the Republican Party since the mid 1800s, their success within it was slow to come. "Abe Lincoln's party" (the Republican Party) dominated American politics throughout the nineteenth century, yet few Swedish Americans held significant positions within it. The party leaders apparently saw little need to coax the Swedish voters with the lure of a political position. Comparatively speaking, Swedish Americans were also less represented in the Civil War than were immigrants from other nations. And in the decades after the war, an impressive military career was almost essential for those who ran for office. Another practical factor that likely kept the Swedish Americans from political positions in those early years was their focus on the enormous task of establishing themselves in their new country.

Hans Mattson, a Swede who had risen to the rank of colonel in the Union Army, was the first of his nationality to become a career politician within state government. Not until 1869 did he get elected to the secretary of state position in Minnesota.

It was not until 1886 that the first Swedish American represented the Republican Party in a national office. John Lind was first elected to the House of Representatives that year; he was reelected twice before he switched party loyalty. In 1898, Lind became Minnesota's Democratic governor.

Charles A. Lindbergh, another Swedish-born politician, was the father of the pilot who flew solo across the Atlantic. He was a Republican who served in the U.S. House of Representatives for five terms between 1906 and 1917. Although he was a member of the Republican Party, he was bold in expressing his disagreements with the leaders of the party.

Like many other Swedish Americans at the time, Lindbergh did not support America's participation in World War I. At the start of the war, most Swedish Americans favored Germany over Sweden's long-term foe, Russia. Lindbergh pushed hard to halt the United States' declaration of war on Germany. Lindbergh was one of 14 representatives who voted against the Armed Ships Bill; 403 voted in favor. This act of individualism, typical of the representative, seemed to seal his political fate; he was never elected to political office again.

Since 1905, Scandinavian-American politicians have met with great success in Minnesota, where the overwhelming majority of governors have been of Scandinavian descent. It is interesting that no Swedish American has ever served as governor of Illinois. Typically, the Swedes have seen more political success in their home states than on a national level.

SOCIAL REFORMS

In the early part of the twentieth century, many Swedish Americans from both the Republican and Democratic parties favored progressive social legislation. It is difficult to know whether their convictions were related to Sweden's legislative reform of the early 1870s. The newly reorganized Riksdag had enacted laws that protected factory workers. Among other things, these laws restricted the number of hours that women and children could work, and they offered workers accident insurance. Sweden was well ahead of most other industrialized nations that considered these social reforms too progressive.

Parties that grew out of progressivism include the Populist Party of the late nineteenth century, the Progressive Party of 1912, and the Farmer-Labor Party of the 1920s. None survived into the twenty-first century, but most of their demands, such as the eight-hour workday and an income tax based on earnings, eventually became law. This movement, especially powerful in Minnesota and Wisconsin, influenced elections.

SWEDISH-LANGUAGE
NEWSPAPERS AND LITERATURE

Almost from the beginning of their immigration to America, the Swedes depended on newspapers to help preserve their culture. These Swedish-language newspapers published letters from newly settled immigrants who sang the praises of America. They became important, too, as forums for rallying fellow Swedish Americans to the cause of preserving their native language and heritage. During the years of mass immigration in the late 1800s, over 1,000 different Swedish-American newspapers were published in 30 states across America. They not only reported the news, but also announced and advertised social and political events that unified Swedish Americans and kept their native identity alive.

The first of these newspapers was published in 1851 and named the *Skandinavien*. It did not live a long life but was the start of a long line of Swedish-American papers. The *Hemlandet Det Gamla och Det Nya (The Old and the New Homeland)* began publication in Galesburg, Illinois, in 1855. T. N. Hasselquist, a Swedish Lutheran pastor from the Augustana Synod, published this paper. It served as a forum for the American Swedish Lutheran churches.

In 1866, the first liberal alternative to the religious newspapers, the *Svenska Amerikanaren* (Swedish American) was published in Chicago. Individualistic intellects such as Magnus Elmblad, O. A. Linder, and Ernst Skarstedt were among those who published the secular papers.

The publishers of the secular papers, revolting against the social constraints that bound them in Sweden, pressed for a Swedish-American, rather than a Swedish, identity for their people. They resisted the desire of many Swedish Americans to set themselves apart from other ethnic groups. Preserving every aspect of their Swedish heritage did not make sense to these publishers. The secular papers competed fiercely against the *Hemlandet* and other church-sponsored papers.

The secular and church-sponsored Swedish-language papers suffered negatively in the years leading up to and after World War I. The pressure across the United States to Americanize led to the loss of subscriptions and in some cases to business failures. By the end of mass emigration in 1930, most of these papers were extinct. Although first-generation Swedish Americans continued to look to the Swedish-language papers for news of their native country, second- and third-generation Swedish Americans were less interested and were unskilled in reading Swedish. The more the Swedish immigrants and their descendants blended into American society, the less need they had for the Swedish-language papers. Today, only a handful survive.

Literature, like journalism, also served as a connector between the old life of Swedish Americans and their new one. And Swedes were among the first cultures to tell stories. Their story-telling tradition dated back to the days of the Nordic gods and the Vikings. Swedish Americans found America to be a good audience for the written word and their unique literature. In the early 1900s, over 300 Swedish-American authors were writing plays, novels, poetry, and short stories. Collectively, these writers were not known for the quality of literature they produced, but they did provide important insights into the life of the immigrants.

Swedish-American prose authors often used their imaginations to describe what life would be like for the immigrant who returned to Sweden. Typically, these authors were balanced in their effort to show both the positive and negative changes that had occurred in Sweden since the immigrants had left.

The Lutheran Augustana Book Concern, established in 1884 in Rock Island, Illinois, was a prominent publisher among Swedish-language publishers. Much of the published material was devotional work or items reprinted from Sweden's prose and poetry.

Swedish-language literature was effective in preserving the Swedish language for decades. But eventually English-language literature began to compete with it. By 1920, Swedish-American literature was losing ground, and after 1937, the Augustana Book Concern was publishing only a few textbooks and magazines in the Swedish language.

Increasingly, Swedish-American authors published in both English and Swedish. Most of those who did publish in English did not write as preservationists of their Swedish heritage. This transition mirrored the loss of Swedish Americans' unique ethnic identity.

The Norrlander's Sighing for Home

The following poem was written by E. Sehlstedt and excerpted from the book *Masterpieces from Swedish Literature*, which was published in 1906 by the Augustana Book Concern in Rock Island, Illinois. The poem, originally printed in the Swedish language, reveals the anguish many Swedish immigrants experienced when they chose to leave their native land, family, and all that was familiar.

The Norrlander's Sighing for Home

Thou longest again for they ancestors' shore!
My heart, how uneasy thou beatest!
When early remembrance of childhood broods o'er
The vales of thy homestead, the sweetest.
In vain thou regretest those wishes of yore,
Which mockingly drove thee to this foreign shore,
From thy dear lovely forests and valleys.

What dreams didst thou dream of the far foreign earth,
To change thus thy home for another?
Wert thou seeking for hearts? Were not such in the north?
Where found'st thou more faithful a brother?
Which dictated hope? Wert thou longing for gold?
What sawest thou there which thou didst not behold
In thy own lovely forests and valleys?

SWEDISH-AMERICAN LUTHERANS' CONNECTION TO SWEDISH STATE CHURCH

Although Sweden's state church paid little attention to any Swedish-American churches, the Swedish-American Lutherans remained more closely connected to Sweden than any of the other Swedish-American churches. This was due to the emigration by the clergymen of the state church. Lars P. Esbjorn was among the most notable members of the former state

Oh, yet I remember my home by the flood,
Where clouds on the mountain-peaks rested;
Where round the low cottage the brave ancient wood
Its shield 'gainst the polar storms tested;
Where life was so harmless, so peaceful and bright,
At the first break of day or the twilight of night,
In my dear lovely forests and valleys.

At rest is my father. The murmuring wave
Sings softly its lullaby for him;
And the white birches grow round the loved one's low grave,
And braid their green foliage o'er him;
But the home of my childhood stands still in its bloom,
And my mother and friends, they still call me to come
To their own lovely forests and valleys.

I'll come from afar ere my course shall be run,
To embrace you once more, ye true-hearted!
But happly [*sic*] too late shall the heart-broken son
Seek the graves of the loved ones departed;
And stand there neglected, forlorn, and alone,
Bemoaning those days of delight which have flown
In his own lovely forests and valleys.

Translated from the original Swedish by N. A. Carlson

A celebrity in Sweden, opera star Jenny Lind lived briefly in America. Lind is seen here in a photo portrait from 1850.

church clergy to leave Sweden. He emigrated with other Lutheran pietists (persons devoted to personal experience in religion) in 1849. The pietists, unlike Sweden's Lutheran Church, placed more importance on a personal reverence for God than on religious formality.

Esbjorn traveled extensively to preach and raise funds for his first church. Among those who donated was Jenny Lind, Sweden's famous opera star, who lived briefly in America. By

1854, the first Swedish-American Lutheran church was built. Esbjorn's leadership resulted in the establishment of Lutheran churches across the Midwest. The Augustana Synod was founded in 1860 as the result of a merger between Swedish and Norwegian churches. By 1870, the Norwegians left the synod to form their own, but the Augustana Synod survived to become the largest Swedish-American denomination. In 1860, about 20 percent of the Swedish-American population were members of this synod; by 1910, representation grew to one-third.

The Swedish Evangelical Covenant church was the second-largest Swedish-American congregation. This church was similar to the Augustana Synod since the Pietist Movement also influenced it. After these members initially joined and then left the Augustana Synod, they went on to establish their own identity in 1885.

Unlike the Augustana Synod and the Swedish Evangelical Covenant churches that began to establish themselves in Sweden, the Swedish-American Baptists and Methodists were further removed from the Swedish state church. These congregations were products of American missionary work in Sweden. They developed after they had immigrated to America.

SWEDISH LANGUAGE GIVES WAY

Swedish was at first the official language of all of the Swedish churches. Over time, there was heated discourse over the question of whether English should be adopted as the official language of the churches or whether Swedish should continue in that honorable capacity. Before the 1880 flood of Swedish immigrants into America, many Swedes were resigned to the fact that English would eventually win out.

The immigrants who belonged to the free churches and the Augustana Synod were viewed as being of a lower class than the rest of the Swedish-American church members. As immigrants found material success, some chose to join the more affluent churches such as the American Episcopal Church.

Even into the late 1800s, the Swedish language held tight in Swedish-American communities. This was a barrier to Swedish Americans as they tried to become American. Because of the husband's daily contact with English-speaking Americans, he typically became the first to speak English. The children were next because of their exposure to English in school. Swedish-American women, except for maids who worked in American homes, were traditionally the last to become bilingual.

By 1900, however, one in every five Swedes lived in America. The significant presence of the Swedes changed their opinion on the matter. The largest share of Swedish Christians wanted to retain their native tongue as the language of their churches. Those in the minority, who disagreed, felt that the future of Swedish-American churches hinged on their ability to attract generations of younger Swedes who were not fluent in the language of their ancestors. To them, this meant that churches would need to adopt English. Between 1900 and 1914, this disagreement became increasingly heated. Despite the pressure for resolution, the Swedish-American churches never reached consensus on this issue on their own. Instead, pressures outside the churches drove this issue to its conclusion.

World War I created a social condition that caused Americans to consider all other organizations, cultures, and languages suspect. By 1925, clergymen in the Augustana Synod delivered services in English. Within 10 years, English was accepted as the official language in all American Lutheran churches. In 1962, the Augustana Synod merged with a German Lutheran church to form the Lutheran Church of America. This union marked the assimilation (incorporation) of the Swedish Church.

Often the Swedish-American churches established schools across the frontier. Even after public schools were opened, Swedish Americans continued to send their children for religious training in the Swedish language. In the public school system, the children's instruction was in English. The children who were caught reverting to the Swedish language at recess were typically punished. While this discipline furthered the English language, it did nothing to further the pride of young Swedes in their heritage.

SWEDISH THEOLOGICAL SEMINARIES

Augustana College in Rock Island, Illinois, was established in 1858 by Lars P. Esbjorn to address the need for new pastors in the Augustana Synod. Esbjorn journeyed to Sweden in 1862 to raise funds for the college, but never returned to America. T. N. Hasselquist became Augustana's first president and assumed Esbjorn's duties.

The other Swedish-American denominations followed Augustana's lead and established theological seminaries of their own. These seminaries eventually transitioned into undergraduate colleges. The Mission Covenant founded North Park College and Seminary in Chicago. Through a merger, the Swedish Baptists formed Bethel College and Seminary in Minneapolis. The Swedish Methodists established what eventually became Kendall College in Evanston, Illinois.

Other colleges that were founded by regional conferences of the Augustana Synod include Upsala College in New Jersey, Gustavus Adolphus College in Minnesota, Luther College in Nebraska, and Bethany College in Kansas. Although all of these schools have retained only a portion of the Swedish influence that founded them, they symbolize the positive side of Swedish assimilation into the American culture.

SWEDISH NATIONAL ORGANIZATIONS

The organizations formed by Swedish Americans typically represented their need to preserve their ethnic identity. Many of the local aid societies eventually merged with national federations. Their purpose was to help the immigrants become self-sufficient, based on a system of health and life insurance premiums.

One of the largest Swedish national organizations, the Vasa Order of America, had as its charter: "To render aid to sick members of the corporation, whether such sickness to be temporary or incurable, and to render pecuniary aid towards defraying the funeral expenses of members, and to promote social and intellectual fellowships among its members." The Vasa Order, started in 1896, the Independent Order of Vikings, founded in 1890, and the Independent Order of Svithiod, established in 1880, eventually shifted from their initial focus. In time, their energies and resources were directed more toward the preservation of their Swedish heritage and traditions. While they continue to manage care facilities for the aged, most of their activities include Swedish education, music, and dance classes. The Vasa Order of America still exists today, although its membership is almost half of what it was in 1929, when Swedish culture was at its peak.

The Swedish Americans' pride in their heritage did not take hold until their immigration to America. America's rise as a world leader at the turn of the century and the celebration of heritage by other European immigrants led to the Swedes' nationalistic sentiment. Although most Swedish Americans also expressed American patriotism, they were especially honored to think that they brought to America all the best that Sweden had to offer.

FRICTION BETWEEN SECULAR AND RELIGIOUS SOCIETIES

Within the Chicago Swedish-American community especially, the friction felt between the classes back in Sweden reemerged. Tension existed between the secular and the religious societies. The typical immigrant who came from Sweden's lower-class rural areas traditionally joined a religious society. They took advantage of the charitable organizations, hospitals, and schools that came with membership. The middle-class immigrants from Sweden's urban areas were more likely to become

Organizations like the Vasa Order and the Independent Order of Vikings, initially established to provide community support and care for the ill, later stressed the preservation of Swedish dance, music, and education. Here, folk dancers celebrate the visit of Sweden's King Carl to America in 1977.

members of the secular societies. These offered cultural and social entertainment. Members of the Augustana Synod saw those in the secular societies as being carryovers from the Swedish middle-class society. Members of the secular societies were put off by what they saw as intolerance for people not aligned with the synod.

The earliest immigrants found it especially tough to learn the English language. The young Swedish Americans learned the language of their adopted country more readily than did their parents and grandparents. This caused tension between the generations. The youth balked at their elders' conservatism, while the elders worried that the youth would ignore their Swedish heritage. World War I brought this issue to a close when legislation was introduced that discouraged all immigrants from using their native tongue. Within and outside the home, English became the primary language of Swedish-Americans by the 1930s.

True to form, the Augustana Synod and the *Hemlandet* criticized those who pushed Americanization. They saw the Swedish language as key not only to preserving their heritage but also to the success of their education programs. The synod had support on this issue from Vilhelm Lundstrom. Lundstrom, respected philologist and a professor at Gothenburg University, believed in the need to preserve Swedish culture even on the American side of the Atlantic. In 1925, he expressed his frustration in several Swedish newspapers:

> Once the will to remain Swedish has died out within the Augustana Synod, it will have betrayed its historic mission, and it will then be swallowed up by a common Anglo-American Lutheranism, in which every trace of Swedish tradition will soon be swept away. . . . Sweden's church is indissolubly bound up with Swedish language and Swedish culture, and with their preservation and cultivation in the world. . . . If Augustana breaks with *that* tradition, it breaks with the church of our fathers . . . [and] with its own proud past.

The *Svenska Amerikanaren,* on the other hand, stressed the importance of the Swedish Americans' assimilation into American society. A sure sign of the Swedes assimilation into American culture was the Americanization of their names. As early as colonial times, John Mortanson, whose signature is on the Declaration of Independence, changed his last name to Morton. Similarly, the Johanssons became the Johnsons or the Jensens; the Nilssons became the Nielsons, and so on.

REACTION OF AMERICANS TO SWEDES

America's reaction to the incoming Swedes varied. Americans usually welcomed the Swedes because they provided the expanding country with practical skills and labor, but many viewed the Swedish as working-class immigrants who would not advance from their social standing. One writer described those immigrants he saw arrive at Castle Garden in 1882. After he harshly criticizes the incoming Italians, Jews, Russians, and the English, he describes the meekness of the Swedish immigrants: "Here come . . . the quiet, modest group of Swedes, true-hearted tillers of the soil, in coats that bear the mark of the parish tailor, and demure women with flaxen hair and light blue eyes."

In contrast, an 1887 history of a Pennsylvania county appraised the Swedes negatively: "Of some of the later immigrants of these [Scandinavian] nationalities little in praise can be said. Coming as common day laborers, with no apparent ambition, they have brought their skepticism and drinking habits with them and are not infrequently found in the criminal courts."

Hans Mattson, a prominent Swedish-American states-man in the late 1800s, understands his countrymen in quite different terms in his memoirs. "Our people in this country did certainly earn a name for integrity and honesty among their American neighbors, which has been a greater help to them than money." Although certainly not unbiased in his feelings, Mattson expressed the opinion of many Americans toward the Swedish.

7 INTO THE MELTING POT:
The Swedish-American Influence

SWEDISH IMMIGRANTS' CONTRIBUTIONS TO AMERICA

Initially, immigrants from Sweden were not well respected, but their significant contributions to their adopted homeland eventually became apparent. After the American Civil War, large numbers of Swedish Americans helped build America's first railroads. They laid track from St. Paul and Chicago first. Later, as the frontier pushed westward, they worked on lines farther west. The linking of America's east and west coasts provided immigrants with a convenient form of transportation and allowed them to settle across the vast United States territories.

In October 1871, four square miles (10 square kilometers) of the city of Chicago burned in the Great Chicago Fire for over two days. Two-hundred-fifty people lost their lives, and 90,000 lost their homes. The city was soon rebuilt; so much of it by the Swedish Americans that people said, "the Swedes built Chicago."

The fact that the Swedish immigrants arrived in America with skills in farming, mining, fishing, logging, and construction meant that they were immediately valuable in helping to tame America's primitive territories. Before the masses of Swedish immigrants poured into America in the mid 1800s, the

After the Chicago fire of 1871, much of the work of rebuilding the city went to Swedish-American laborers. In addition to being adept builders, Swedes were also known for their skill as loggers, miners, and fishermen.

territories of Kansas, Illinois, and Nebraska were empty prairies. Minnesota, Wisconsin, North and South Dakota, and Manitoba and Saskatchewan, Canada, were primarily forests with few inhabitants. Washington, Alaska, and British Columbia, Canada, were populated with only dense woodlands; no one lived there.

By the end of the nineteenth century, with help from German and Norwegian immigrants, entire towns and cities had been established. The Swedish Americans were essential to this development. They led the way in cutting trees, breaking up sod, farming, and forming communities. American and Canadian settlements were established all the way to the West Coast by the time they had finished. And, collectively, Swedish Americans broke more ground in America than was cultivated in all of Sweden. In helping to expand America's borders to include over three million square miles, the immigrants helped transform it into one of the strongest nations in the world.

Swedish immigrants from the forestlands in northern Sweden introduced log cabins to North America. These sturdy homes were a vast improvement from the crude "soddies" that were typically their first homes.

Olaf Krans, a Swedish immigrant who journeyed to the Bishop Hill, Illinois, settlement with his parents in 1850, introduced Americans to a unique Swedish immigrant type of folk art. When he reached his fifties, Krans began to paint scenes of what he remembered about growing up in that religious community. His pictures are of women and men sowing and reaping; they show settlers breaking up the prairie and working to create a unique enclave of their own (an example of Krans' work appears on page 48). His work is currently displayed at Bishop Hill State Historic Site.

Another significant contribution of the Swedish immigrants to America was the establishment of free churches across the country. The impact of the Swedish-American religious communities is far-reaching and enduring. They established institutions of higher learning, charitable organizations, and publishing companies. Important from the beginning, these institutions represented the need to separate church and state.

THE CONTRIBUTION OF SWEDISH IMMIGRANTS TO SWEDEN

In considering the contributions of the Swedish immigrants, it is important to note the part they played in transforming not only America, but also their native land. Had the immigrants never left Sweden, their motherland would likely have devolved

Notable Swedish Americans

John Ericsson (1803–1889) was born in Värmland, Sweden. An inventor and engineer, Ericsson went to America in 1839 and was most famous for designing the Union Army's *Monitor*—the first ironclad battleship ever made.

Alfred Nobel (1833–1896) was born in Stockholm, Sweden, and studied mechanical engineering in Russia and the United States. As a chemist and inventor, he developed explosives under his father's leadership. His development of dynamite made him a wealthy man. His misgivings for creating a weapon of destruction led him to set up a philanthropic fund. Each year monetary awards, Nobel Prizes, are given out for accomplishments in various disciplines.

Selma Lagerlof (1858–1940) was a novelist and Nobel laureate who was born in Marbacka, Sweden. Her novels and short stories dealt with Swedish life of the past. In 1909, she became the first woman to win the Nobel Prize in literature.

Charles R. Walgreen (1873–1939) was born in Knox County, near Galesburg, Illinois, to Swedish parents. He started his career working in a shoe factory, where he ended up injuring his hand. After quitting that position, he took a job in a drug store. By 1901, he had opened up his own drug store in Chicago. Today, there are almost 4,000 Walgreen's stores throughout the United States and Puerto Rico.

Carl Sandburg (1878–1967) was born in Galesburg, Illinois, to Swedish immigrant parents. A poet and biographer, he was best known for his six-volume biography of Abraham Lincoln. He held jobs as a milk driver, soldier in the Spanish-American War, farmer, and salesman before he became a journalist and poet. He earned a reputation for being a realist who was concerned about the ordinary men and women who were part of urban industrial life.

Notable Swedish Americans *(continued)*

Joel Hagglund, a.k.a. Joe Hill (1879–1915) was born in Gavle, Sweden and immigrated to America in 1902. Joel, who Americanized his name to Joe Hill, joined the Industrial Workers of the World union in 1910 and became an activist. His dream was that the union brotherhood would bring justice to the laborers. Joe's dream ended when he was accused of murder. He was put to death in 1915 for the crime, though many suspected those who feared his increasing power within the union framed him.

Charles Lindbergh (1902–1974) was born in Detroit, Michigan, and grew up in Minnesota. He was an American aviator, engineer, and Pulitzer Prize winner. The son of a Swedish-American mother and politician father, he was the first person to fly nonstop from New York to Paris. His flight lasted 33 hours and 32 minutes. He won a Pulitzer Prize for writing an autobiography that was titled after the plane that gained him fame, "The Spirit of St. Louis."

Greta Garbo (1905–1990) was born Greta Gustaffson in Stockholm, Sweden. Though born into poverty, she was educated at the Royal Dramatic Theaters' school of acting. In the early 1920s, she accompanied her director, Mauritz Stiller, to Hollywood, where she stayed and became one of the most popular stars of her time. She was known as the "Swedish Sphinx." She became a United States citizen in 1951.

into a slum, bogged down by far-reaching poverty. Considering the country's overpopulation issue in the mid 1800s, wages and the general standard of living for most Swedes would have remained low. Unemployment and welfare problems would have run rampant.

The emigrants' departure helped ease Sweden's catastrophic population troubles, while the money they sent back to Sweden strengthened its economy. An average of $8 million a year was sent to Sweden by Swedish-American relatives between 1906 and 1930.

Ironically, many of the reforms that helped transform Sweden into the strong and stable country it is today were due to emigration. The Swedish government eventually studied the emigration phenomenon and understood what drove so many from their country. In both Sweden and America, the Swedish immigrants came to command respect for the self-made man.

SWEDISH-AMERICAN POPULATION

Currently, Minnesota still has the highest population of Swedish Americans—so many that it is sometimes referred to as the "Swedish state." The states of Washington, Nebraska, North and South Dakota, Oregon, Idaho, Utah, Montana, Wyoming, and Iowa also have large concentrations of Swedish Americans. The 1990 United States Census shows that 40 percent of those who claimed Swedish ancestry are living in the Midwest. Thirty-two percent live in the West, about 14 percent live in the Northeast, and 14 percent live in the South. As Swedish Americans age, many relocate to the milder climates in the southern and the western parts of the country.

The 2000 United States Census statistics show that 4,339,357 people identified themselves as having a Swedish heritage; most of those, 98 percent, were born in the United States. According to 1990 figures, the largest share of Swedish Americans currently works in technical, sales, and administrative positions (33.3 percent) or in managerial and professional positions (32.8 percent). About 10.5 percent work in service positions, and the same percentage work as operators, fabricators, and laborers. It is interesting to note that 2.8 percent , the smallest portion of Swedish Americans, are currently employed in farming, forestry, and fishing positions.

CURRENT IMMIGRATION

As the statistics show, very few Swedes have immigrated to America in recent decades. The conditions in Sweden that launched the Swedish emigration in the nineteenth century no longer exist. Sweden is virtually free from the problems that plagued it over a century ago. And what attracted the early immigrants to America no longer exists either; this is especially true as it applies to the availability of acres and acres of cheap land.

Migration between America and Sweden was reduced even more dramatically after World War II than it was after World War I. Only about 50,000 Swedish immigrated to the United States between 1931 and 1970. That number has been even lower since 1971.

Swedish immigrants arriving since World War II are an entirely different breed than their predecessors. Many are professionals and skilled technicians. Typically, they are sophisticated and well educated. They, much more than the early Swedish immigrants, are fully enmeshed in their national culture. Many who relocate here today retain their Swedish citizenship; they do not consider themselves Swedish Americans but Swedes living in America. The third generation of Swedish Americans now are fully assimilated into American society. Many have expressed a new pride in and a curiosity about their Swedish heritage.

CONTINUATION OF SWEDISH CULTURE

The desire to celebrate the Swedish culture stretches beyond individuals and into Swedish-American organizations. Among those that still exist today is the Vasa Order of America. The Order is named after Gustav Vasa, who is considered the king of modern Sweden. What began as a fraternal society for Swedish immigrants over 100 years ago has grown to meet the new needs of Scandinavian Americans. Initially, Vasa members looked to the organization to help them learn about America. Now, Vasa provides a way for these Scandinavian Americans to remember or learn the culture of the "old country." Vasa members encourage the observation of special dates such as Leif Ericksson Day and Midsummer. Festivities include Scandinavian music and smorgasbord. In the United States, Sweden, and Canada, over 300 Vasa Order lodges still exist. The Swedish Colonial Society was founded in 1909 and is the

According to the 2000 U.S. Census, over four million Americans identify themselves as having Swedish heritage. Though Swedish immigration has greatly declined since the 1800s, many examples of Sweden's rich cultural traditions survive.

For Swedes, the start of the Christmas season is marked by Saint Lucia's Day on December 13. The holiday honors a young girl who was killed for her Christian beliefs in the fourth century. In the traditional ceremony, a young girl is crowned with a wreath of lit candles.

oldest Swedish historical organization in America. Initially, the society existed to document the history of the first colonial Swedish settlement in America. The society strives to collect, preserve, and publish materials that are connected to the history of Swedish and Finnish Americans. The organization maintains parks, memorials of historic sites, and monuments. They also commemorate historic events. These organizations, like third-generation Swedish Americans, help keep alive the traditions that were brought to America by their forefathers.

The celebration of holidays is one important way Swedish Americans keep Swedish traditions alive. The Swedish Christmas season begins with St. Lucia's Day on December 13.

The holiday honors a young girl who was killed for her Christian beliefs in the fourth century. In Swedish and Swedish-American families, one of the daughters dresses as St. Lucia in a white dress and her head crowned with a wreath of lit candles. "St. Lucia" sings traditional songs and serves coffee and pastries to family members as they awake. The lit candles symbolize light returning to a dark earth.

On Christmas Eve, the high point of the 20-day celebration, dinner includes lutfisk, which is cod soaked in lye, and rice porridge. The Swedish Santa, Jultomten, delivers gifts to the children. Typical ornaments are made of straw and bound with ribbons. These ornaments vary in shape, but many are formed into the shape of goats. Christmas Day is devoted to reverent reflection and an early morning church service called Julotta. The Swedes typically visit neighbors on December 26.

Traditional Swedish foods that continue to be enjoyed in America even today include Swedish pancakes topped with lingonberries and Swedish meatballs, which are served in onions and sour cream. And, of course, everyone's favorite, the smorgasbord, is a feasting table filled with a variety of hot and cold dishes. This Swedish tradition has become, just like those Swedish immigrants who introduced it, a part of the fabric of America.

50 B.C.	Swedish tribes begin trading with the Roman Empire.
A.D. 829	St. Ansgar introduces Christianity in Sweden.
800–1000s	Swedish Vikings establish colonies and trade routes in other countries.
1397	The Kalmar Union united Sweden with Denmark and Norway under Margaret I.
1435	The Riksdag, the law-making governmental body, is established.
1523	Sweden becomes independent under King Gustav I. He later establishes Lutheranism as the state religion.
1638	The first Swedes colonize in America.
1709	Peter the Great of Russia defeats Swedish forces. Swedish power in Europe soon declines.
1720	A new constitution grants many of the crown's powers to the Riksdag, beginning the "Age of Liberty." Royal power is not reestablished until 1772.
1840	Swedish emigration law changes, allowing its citizens to leave.
1840–1864	First major wave of Swedes immigrate to America.
1841	Gustav Unonius declares himself the "first emigrant."
1845	Religious leader Erik Jansson immigrates to America.
1846	Erik Jansson and 1,200 followers establish the Bishop Hill community in Illinois.
1848	Gold is discovered at Sutters Mill; the California Gold Rush follows in 1849.
1849	Pastor Esbjorn establishes the Swedish Lutheran Church in America in Andover, Illinois.
1855	The Castle Garden landing station opens in New York.
1857–1859	American economic depression.
1860s	The Swedish birthrate declines.
1861–1865	American Civil War. British and German shipping firms produce steamships designed to carry passengers.
1862	United States passes the Homestead Act that offers free land to its citizens and to those who plan to declare themselves citizens. The Sioux Indian Uprising in Minnesota.

1865-1889	The second wave of Swedes immigrate to America.
1866	After this time, Swedish religious and cultural institutions begin to develop rapidly in America.
1867–1869	Severe crop failures in Sweden.
1868	Hans Mattson begins to serve as an agent for the American Railroad.
1873	American economic depression.
1884	Augustana Book Concern, a Swedish-language publisher, is established.
1887	John Lind is elected as the first Swedish-American congressman.
1890–1914	Third major wave of Swedish immigrants voyage to America.
1890	Minneapolis replaces Chicago as main urban destination for Swedish immigrants.
1892	Sweden's military conscription is increased to 90 days.
1893	American economic depression.
1896–1900	Klondike Gold rush in Alaska and the Yukon territory.
1908	Sweden publishes the *Report of the Commission on Emigration*. The report reveals the grievances of the poorer classes against the Swedish government and society. Reforms follow quickly.
1910	Swedish-born population in America is at its peak.
1914–1918	World War I.
1920	By the end of the decade, about 1.5 million Swedes live in the United States.
1921	American economic downturn.
1924	America passes legislation that restricts immigration.
1930	Great Depression in America.
1939–1945	World War II.

Barton, H. Arnold. *Letters from the Promised Land.* Minneapolis: University of Minnesota Press, 1975.

Barton, H. Arnold. *A Folk Divided: Homeland Swedes and Swedish Americans.* Carbondale: Southern Illinois University Press, 1994.

Carley, Kenneth. *Minnesota in the Civil War: An Illustrated History.* St. Paul: Minnesota Historical Society Press, 2000.

Hillbrand, Percie V. *Swedes in America.* Minneapolis: Lerner Publications Company, 1966.

Johansson, Carl-Erik. *Cradled in Sweden.* Logan, Utah: Everton Publishers, 1995.

Kastrup, Allan. *The Swedish Heritage in Minnesota.* St. Paul, Minnesota: North Central Publishing Company, 1975.

Koustrup, Soren. *Shattered Dreams: Joe Hill.* Mankato, Minnesota: Creative Education, 1982.

Lewis, Anne Gillespie. *So Far Away in the World: Stories from the Swedish Twin Cities.* Minneapolis: Nodin Press, 2002.

Ljungmark, Lars. *Swedish Exodus.* Carbondale, Illinois: Southern Illinois University Press, 1979.

Malmberg, Carl. *America Is Also Scandinavian.* New York: G. P. Putnam and Sons, 1970.

McGill, Allyson. *The Swedish Americans.* Philadelphia: Chelsea House Publishers, 1997.

Microsoft Encarta Encyclopedia 1999.

Mihelich, Josephine. *Andrew Peterson and the Scandia Story.* Minneapolis: Ford Johnson Graphics, 1984.

Olson, Kay Melchisedech. *Norwegian, Swedish, and Danish Immigrants.* Mankato, Minnesota: Capstone Press, 2002.

Paddock, Lisa and Carl Rollyson. *A Student's Guide to Scandinavian American Genealogy.* Phoenix, Arizona: The Rosen Publishing Group, 1996.

Robbins, Albert. *Coming to America: Immigrants from Northern Europe.* New York: Delacorte Press, 1981.

Runblom, Harald and Hans Norman. *From Sweden to America: A History of the Migration.* Minneapolis: University of Minnesota Press, 1976.

Barton, H. Arnold. *Letters from the Promised Land: Swedes in America, 1840–1914*. Minneapolis: University of Minnesota Press, 1975.

Bjorn, Thyra Ferra. *Papa's Wife*. New York: Holt, Rinehart & Winston, 1956.

Hasselmoe, Nils. *Swedish America, an Introduction*. Minneapolis: Brings Press, 1976.

Kastrup, Allan. *The Swedish Heritage in America*. St. Paul, Minnesota: North Central Publishing Company for the Swedish Council of America, 1975.

Ljungmark, Lars. *Swedish Exodus*. Trans. Kermit B. Westerberg. Carbondale and Edwardsville, Illinois: Southern Illinois University Press for the Swedish Pioneer Historical Society, 1979.

McGill, Allyson. *The Swedish Americans*. Philadelphia: Chelsea House, 1997.

Mihelich, Josephine. *Andrew Peterson and the Scandia Story*. Minneapolis, Minnesota: author and Ford Johnson Graphics, 1984.

Moberg, Vilhelm. *The Emigrants*. Trans. Gustaf Lannestock. London: Max Reinhardt, 1956.

Paddock, Lisa and Carl Rollyson. *A Student's Guide to Scandinavian Genealogy*. Phoenix, Arizona: The Rosen Publishing Group, 1996.

Sandburg, Carl. *Always the Young Strangers*. New York: Harcourt Brace, 1965.

The Swedish Information Smorgasbord
http://www.sverigeturism.se/smorgasbord

The Swenson Center – Swedish Immigration and Research
http://www.augustana.edu/administration/swenson/

Swedish Council of America
http://www.swedishcouncil.org

The American Family Immigration History Center at Ellis Island
http://www.ellisisland.org

American West – European Emigration
http://www.americanwest.com/swedemigr/pages/emigra.htm

Immigration History Research Center at the University of Minnesota
http://www1.umn.edu/ihrc

Swedish Migration
http://www.anthro.mankato.msus.edu/history/mnstatehistory/swedish_migration.html

The American Swedish Institute
2600 Park Ave.
Minneapolis, MN 55407

Consulate General of Sweden
One Dag Hammarskjold Plaza
New York, NY 10017-2210

Swedish American Museum Center
5211 North Clark Street
Chicago, IL 60640

Swedish Colonial Society
371 Devon Way
West Chester, PA 19380

The American Swedish Historical Museum
1900 Pattison Ave.
South Philadelphia, PA 19145

The American-Scandinavian Foundation
58 Park Avenue
New York, NY 10016

Swedish Genealogical Group
c/o Minnesota Genealogical Society
P.O. Box 16069
St. Paul, MN 55116-0069

Family History Library of the
Church of Jesus Christ of Latter-Day Saints
35 North West Temple Street
Salt Lake City, UT 84150

National Genealogical Society
4527 Seventeenth Street North
Arlington, VA 22207-2399

Acceptance into America
and clash with Swedish values, 59
and number of Swedes, 19, 89
and reaction of Americans to
Swedes, 83
See also Assimilation
Agents, and propaganda to immigrants,
36, 38
Alaska, Swedes in, 39, 86
America Fever, 38
America letters, and emigration, 38, 59
Ansgar, Saint, 22
Anti-Swedish sentiment
and Indian massacres, 52-53, 55, 59
and World War I, 19
Asgar Synod, 64
Assimilation, 74
and colleges, 79
and English language, 77-79, 82
and friction between secular and
religious societies, 80-83
and religion, 78
and third generation Swedish
Americans, 90
Augustana Book Concern, 65, 72,
73, 74
Augustana College, 79
Augustana Lutheran Synod, 48, 64,
65, 72, 77, 78, 79, 81, 82

Baptists, in U.S., 64, 77, 79
Bethany College, 79
Bethel College and Seminary, 79
Bishop Hill, 47, 86
Black Death, 23
Bloodbath of Stockholm, 24

California, Swedes in, 14, 33, 39, 50
Canada, Swedes in, 86
Canal boats, for journey to Midwest,
47
Castle Garden, 43, 45-46, 51, 83
Catholicism, in Sweden, 22-23, 24
Chicago, Swedes in, 16, 18, 39, 49,
60, 79

Children
and English language, 78-79
and life on prairie, 58-59
Cholera, in U.S., 49
Christian, King of Denmark, 24
Christmas, 92-93
Church of Sweden. *See* Lutheranism
Citizenship, and Homestead Act, 32
Civil War, Swedes in, 36, 51, 66-67, 70
Colleges, 79
Conventicle Act, 34

Delaware, Swedes in, 13-14, 24
Democratic Party, 66
Denmark, 23, 24
Diseases
on journey to U.S., 41
in U.S., 49

East, Swedes in, 50, 60, 63
Ellis Island, 43
Elmblad, Magnus, 72
English language, Swedish language
giving way to, 77-79, 82
Episcopal Church, 77
Eric IX, 23
Ericsson, John, 51
Erik of Pomerania, 23
Esbjorn, Reverend Lars P., 48, 75-77,
79
Evangelical Lutheran Mission Synod,
64

Farm communities, on prairie, 59, 86
Farmer-Labor Party, 71
Farmers, Swedes as
in Sweden, 12-13, 14, 16, 23, 26,
27, 29, 32-33, 63
in U.S., 16, 32-33, 39, 50, 59-60,
61-62, 63, 89
Folk art, 86
Food
on journey to U.S., 41
in U.S., 51-52, 93
France, 25-26

Gold Rush, and emigration
  in California, 14, 33, 39
  in Klondike, 39
Gothenburg, emigrants leaving from, 42
Guides, for immigrants, 46
Gustav II Adolph, King, 24
Gustavus Adolphus College, 79
Gustav Vasa, King, 24

Hasselquist, T. N., 72, 79
Health care
  and national organizations, 79-80
  and religious organizations, 64
Hemlandet Det Gamla och Det Nya, 72, 82
Hill, James J., 50
Hokanson, M. F., 48
Holidays, 90, 92-93
Homes, for early Midwest emigrants, 52, 58-59, 86
Homestead Act of 1862, 15-16, 32, 39, 60
Hull, England, emigrants leaving from, 42

Idaho, Swedes in, 89
Illinois, Swedes in, 16, 47, 48-49, 51, 71, 73, 79, 86
Immigration to America
  certification of good standing from parish clergy for, 40-41
  and first immigrant, 38, 47
  and first major wave (1840-1864), 14-16, 32, 38-39, 41, 47-49, 52-53, 55, 57-59, 62, 73
  and first Swedes in colonies, 13-14, 24
  and Gold Rush, 14, 33, 39
  and jobs and wages, 33-34
  and land ownership, 14-16, 23, 27, 32-33, 38, 39, 47, 59-60
  and letter from emigrants, 38, 59
  and military conscription, 16, 26-27, 36, 39
  and number of Swedes, 14, 18-19, 49
  obstacles to, 40-41
  and poverty, 12-13, 16, 27, 29, 33, 39, 40
  in recent decades, 89-91
  and religious freedom, 14, 22-23, 24, 26, 27, 34, 38, 59
  and second major wave (1865-1889), 12-13, 16, 33-34, 38, 39, 49, 51-52, 59-60, 62, 72, 73
  and social structure, 14, 23, 24, 26, 34, 36, 59
  and starvation, 12-13, 16, 39
  and third major wave (1890-1914), 16, 18-19, 38, 39-40, 49, 51-52, 63, 67, 73, 90
  and transportation industry propaganda, 36, 38
Independent Order of Svithiod, 80
Independent Order of Vikings, 80
Indian massacres, 52-53, 55, 59
Industrial Revolution, 50
Influence of Swedish-Americans, 85-90, 92-93
Iowa, Swedes in, 16, 47, 50

Jansson, Erik, 34, 47
Janssonites, 47
Jobs, and emigration, 33-34
Jonsdotter, Maria Helene, 41
Journey to America, 41-43
  food on, 41
  and journey to Midwest, 46-47
  landing stations for, 43, 45-46, 51
  money for, 40
  ports for, 42
  ships for, 41-43

Kalmar Union, 23
Kansas, Swedes in, 47, 50, 79, 86
Kendall College, 79
Klondike Gold Rush, 39
Krans, Olaf, 86

Laborers, Swedes as, 16, 33-34, 40, 50, 59-60, 61-62, 63, 83, 89
Landing stations, 43, 45-46, 51
Land ownership, and emigration, 14-16, 23, 27, 32-33, 38, 39, 47, 59-60, 66
Leif Ericksson Day, 90
Lincoln, Abraham, 15, 51, 66-67, 70
Lind, Jenny, 76
Lind, John, 70
Linder, O. A., 72
Lindbergh, Charles A., 70-71
Literature, and Swedes, 73
Little Crow, 55
Liverpool, England, emigrants leaving from, 42
Log homes, for early Midwest emigrants, 52, 58, 59, 86
Lumberjacks, Swedes as, 32, 50, 58, 60, 62-63
Lundstrom, Vilhelm, 82
Luther, Martin, 24, 34
Lutheran Church of America, 78
Lutheranism
    in Sweden, 14, 24, 26, 27, 34
    in U.S., 47-48, 63-64, 72, 73, 74, 75-79, 82
Luther College, 79

Magnus Ladulas, King, 23
Maids, Swedes as, 16, 39, 62, 78
Margaret I, 23
Massachusetts, Swedes in, 50
Mattson, Hans, 51, 70, 83
Methodists, in U.S., 64, 77, 79
Michigan, Swedes in, 16, 39
Midsummer, 90
Midwest, Swedes in, 16, 39, 46-50, 51-53, 55, 57-59, 60, 62, 64, 70, 71, 73, 79, 85-86, 89
Military conscription, and emigration, 16, 26-27, 36, 39
Miners, Swedes as, 14, 32, 33, 39
Minneapolis, Swedes in, 39, 60, 79
Minnesota, Swedes in, 16, 18, 47, 49, 51, 52-53, 55, 70, 71, 86, 89

Missionaries, for immigrants, 46
Mission Covenant Church, 64, 79
Monitor (Union ship), 51
Montana, Swedes in, 89
Mormons, in U.S., 34, 64
Mortanson, John, 82-83

Names, Americanization of, 82-83
Napoleonic Wars, 25-26
Nebraska, Swedes in, 47, 79, 86, 89
New Jersey, Swedes in, 79
Newspapers, Swedish, 65, 72-73, 82
New Sweden, 13-14, 24
New York City, Swedes in, 50
Nordic religion, 22
North Dakota, Swedes in, 86, 89
Northeast, Swedes in, 89
North Park College and Seminary, 79
Northwest, Swedes in, 50

Occupations, 16, 32-34, 39, 50, 58, 59-60, 62-63, 83, 85-86
    and labor disputes and strikes, 60-62
    since World War II, 89, 90
    and social reforms, 71
    and wages, 63
    and working conditions, 63
Oregon, Swedes in, 89
Oxenstierna, Count Axel, 24

Pacific Northwest, Swedes in, 62-63
Palmquist, Gustav, 64
Parish clergy, certification of good standing from for emigration, 40-41
Parliament Act of 1866, 36
Pennsylvania, Swedes in, 50
Peterson, Andrew, 42-43
Pietist Movement, 76, 77
Political involvement
    and political parties, 66-67, 70, 71
    and social reforms, 71
    and Swedes holding offices, 70-71
    and Swedes in Civil War, 36, 51, 66-67, 70

Political parties, 66-67, 70, 71
Populist Party, 71
Ports, for emigration, 42
Poverty
    and emigration, 27, 29, 33, 39, 40
    in U.S., 49, 51-52
Prairies, Swedes on, 51-53, 55, 58-59, 86
Preemption Law, 32
Princeton (Union ship), 51
Progressive Party, 71
Publications, 72-74, 82
    and religious organizations, 64-65, 72-73, 74
    Swedish, 64-65, 66

Railroads
    and propaganda to immigrants, 36
    and transporting emigrants West, 63
Railroad workers
    and strikes, 60
    Swedes as, 32, 33, 50, 58, 60, 62
Religion
    and emigration, 14, 22-23, 24, 26, 27, 34, 38, 59
    and friction with secular organizations, 80-83
    and Swedish language giving way to English, 77-78
    and theological seminaries, 79
    in U.S., 47-48, 63-66, 72-73, 74, 75-79, 82, 86-87
Republican Party, 66, 70
Revivalist movement, 34
Riksdag, 23-24, 26, 34, 71
Rocky Mountain States, Swedes in, 49-50

St. Lucia's Day, 92-93
St. Paul, Swedes in, 39
Schools
    English language in, 78-79
    and religious organizations, 64, 78, 79

Seasickness, on journey to U.S., 41, 42-43
Secular organizations, 66, 79-83, 90, 92
Settlement patterns
    in cities, 49-50, 63
    and homes, 86
    on prairies, 51-53, 55, 58-59, 86
    and preservation of culture, 16, 18, 61
    in rural areas, 50, 51-52
    in suburbs, 49
Ships, for journey to U.S., 41-43
Sioux Indians, and Swedes, 52-53, 55
Skandinavien (newspaper), 72
Skarstedt, Ernst, 72
Slavery, 36, 66
Social structure, and emigration, 14, 23, 24, 26, 34, 36, 59
Sod homes ("soddies"), for early Midwest emigrants, 52, 58, 86
South, Swedes in, 89
South Dakota, Swedes in, 86, 89
Starvation, and emigration, 12-13, 16, 39
Steamship companies, and propaganda to immigrants, 36
Svenska Amerikanaren, 72, 82
Sweden, 21-27, 29
    and colonization in America, 24
    contribution of Swedish immigrants to, 87-89
    and crop failures, 12-13, 16
    and early conflicts and battles, 24
    and early history, 22-24
    and economy, 25-26
    and language, 22
    and military conscription, 16, 26-27, 39
    and permitting emigration, 14, 29
    and physical features, 21-22
    and population increase, 14, 26, 87-88
    and poverty, 12-13, 16, 26-27, 29, 33, 39, 40

and religion, 22-23, 24, 26, 27, 34, 38

and restrictions on emigration, 14, 39-40

and social reforms, 71

and social structure, 14, 23, 24, 26, 27, 34, 38

Swede Town (Chicago), 49

Swedish-American Lutheran church, first, 48, 76-77

Swedish Baptist Church, 64

Swedish Colonial Society, 90, 92

Swedish Evangelical Mission Covenant of America, 64, 77

Swedish fiddle, 63

Swedish language
  English language overcoming, 77-79, 82
  preservation of, 16, 18, 73-74
  roots of, 22

Swedish Methodist Church, in U.S., 64

Swedish tradition/culture, 16, 18
  and foods, 93
  and holidays, 90, 92-93
  and newer generations, 19
  and publications, 64-65, 66, 72-74, 82
  and recent emigrants, 90
  and religious organizations, 47-48, 63-66, 75-79
  and secular organizations, 66, 79-80, 90, 92

and Swedish language, 16, 18, 73-74, 77-79, 82

and theater, 66

See also Assimilation

Tegne'r, Esaias, 14

Theaters, Swedish, 66

Theological seminaries, 79

Unionius, Gustaf, 38

Upsala College, 79

Utah, Swedes in, 89

Vasa, Gustav, 90

Vasa Order of America, 80, 90

Vikings, 23

Wages, and emigration, 33-34

Warberg, A. Carlsson, 66-67

Washington state, Swedes in, 86, 89

West, Swedes in, 33, 39, 49-50, 62-63, 89

Wisconsin, Swedes in, 71, 86

Women
  and English language, 78
  as maids, 16, 39, 62, 78
  on prairies, 52, 58-59, 86

World War I, 19, 40, 71, 78, 82

Wyoming, Swedes in, 89

Yukon Territory, Swedes in, 39

page:

13: © Bettmann/CORBIS
18: Hulton Archive by Getty Images
21: © Hans Strand/CORBIS
25: Hierophant Collection
31: © CORBIS
37: © Minnesota Historical Society/ CORBIS
42: © Bettmann/CORBIS
45: © CORBIS
48: © Francis G. Mayer/CORBIS
53: © Bettmann/CORBIS

57: © Bettmann/CORBIS
62: © Museum of History & Industry/ CORBIS
65: Hulton Archive by Getty Images
69: © CORBIS
76: Hulton Archive by Getty Images
81: © Owen Franken/CORBIS
85: Hulton Archive by Getty Images
91: © Raymond Gehman/CORBIS
92: Hulton Archive by Getty Images

Cover: © Ted Spiegel/CORBIS

Frontis: Courtesy University of Texas at Austin, Perry-Castañeda Map Collection, CIA map.

"My America" text on page 54 from H. Arnold Barton, editor, *Letters from the Promised Land: Swedes in America, 1840–1914* (University of Minnesota Press, 1975), pp. 250–251, 278–279. Used by permission of the University of Minnesota Press.

CORY GIDEON GUNDERSON is a freelance writer and editor. She has written biographies on historical figures published for library and school markets. Cory thoroughly enjoys researching and writing about people and events from the past. She is motivated by the challenge of making history come alive for students today.

Cory also writes and edits technical books and has written company newsletters, magazine articles, and political campaign literature and speeches.

DANIEL PATRICK MOYNIHAN is a former United States senator from New York. He is also the only person in American history to have served in the cabinets or subcabinets of four successive presidents—Kennedy, Johnson, Nixon, and Ford. Formerly a professor of government at Harvard University, he has written and edited many books.